Praise

'Teenagers are leaving school unprepared for the world of money. Immediately they are prey for high-interest credit cards, student debt, financial scams and the ruthless gig economy. They might have passed all their exams and done well at their after-school hobbies but little of it will have them ready for the real world. Before the internet, young people had time to learn, they were unlikely to be exposed to promotions or "special offers" that could seriously damage their finances. Today's teens can be influenced directly through their social media and their time online. It's deeply important that parents read *Smarter Richer Braver* and apply the messages and strategies it talks about before your kids are able to sign contracts they don't understand. *Smarter Richer Braver* allows parents to get in early and prepare their kids; not only to avoid bad decisions but to begin a lifetime of great choices that will make them secure, successful and wealthier over time.'

— **Daniel Priestley,** founder of Dent Global, entrepreneur and author of *How To Raise Entrepreneurial Kids*

'*Smarter Richer Braver* is the consummate reader's guide to making financial literacy topics accessible to every family and every young person looking to take command of their economic future. Marilyn Pinto has captured the essence of what will work – and what will not – in educating our children to be more financially literate in a challenging world. It is a must-read for parents – and educators.'

> — **Robert G. Badal**, co-founder, Financial
> Literacy Project, Santa Barbara

'In *Smarter Richer Braver*, Marilyn L. Pinto asks excellent questions about teens and money, inspiring us to initiate financial education for the next generation.'

> —**Andrew Hallam**, bestselling author of
> *Millionaire Teacher: The Nine Rules of Wealth*
> *You Should Have Learned at School*

'Teenagers now, more than ever, need to be prepared for a financial future that is uncertain and complex. *Smarter Richer Braver* highlights the need and roadmap to empower them how to embrace their financial future.'

> — **Robert Gardner**, chair of the Children's
> Financial Education Policy Council UK

'Teenagers today need to learn about money. Schools don't do it properly, so teens are learning from the wrong people, including peers who are just as clueless as they are, and financial marketers who want to sell them unsuitable products and services. As Marilyn

Pinto says in *Smarter Richer Braver,* parents have to take responsibility for their children's financial education. Helping teenagers to develop a healthy relationship with money and, crucially, good financial habits, is one of the most valuable things a parent can do for them.'

— **Robin Powell**, journalist, author and editor of
The Evidence-Based Investor

'If you think teaching kids about money isn't important, think again. *Smarter Richer Braver* sets out, in no uncertain terms, why all families need to take action now to make sure their teens grow up financially healthy. I'd recommend to all families who want to change their kids' financial future for the better.'

— **Will Rainey**, author of *Grandpa's Fortune Fables*

'I look back on school with frustration. Why was I never taught about money and finances? Why did nobody explain my options to me? I've always been conscientious, and so I saved my money in low-interest savings accounts in my early twenties, but how much money could my savings have been making me had I known what I know now? I'm so pleased that someone is finally teaching our children and teenagers about how it is in the real world. Why should we expect youngsters to figure it out for themselves? *Smarter Richer Braver* had to be written – thank you Marilyn.

If you're a parent, take the time to read this and help shape a better future for your children.'

— **Neil Fachie, MBE**, fourteen-times World Champion Cyclist and number-one bestselling author of *Earn Your Stripes*

'In a complicated world of money, where hard cash coexists with invisible bitcoins, and where financial decision-making is bounded by a hundred imponderables and confounding situations, an easy guide to understanding finance and economy is hard to come by. It is surprising how, despite the great need and demand for one, the supply of simply written books on financial literacy is abysmal. One reason could be the effort and the meticulousness that must go into producing a manuscript that must at once satisfy the lay person and the academic, the child and the parent, the teacher and the student. Marilyn has performed this miracle and has clearly put her heart and soul into *Smarter Richer Braver*. Looking forward to her next.'

— **Amir Ullah Khan, PhD**, visiting professor, Indian School of Business, Hyderabad (ex-deputy director, Bill and Melinda Gates Foundation)

'The life of a teenager can be tough. Not only do they face more social demands than any generation before them, but they have little-to-no formal introduction to the world of managing money. That's why *Smarter Richer Braver* is such an important book. Let's take financial empowerment off their list of worries.'

— **Sam Instone**, CEO at AES International

'There has never been a time when it is more important for everyone in the world to be aware of how to use money better and become part of the financial system. If we don't make that happen, more and more people will be left behind. Luckily, there has also never been a time when it has been as possible as it is today to reach people with ideas, education and training. Right now, there is an opportunity for us to leap forward decades and change the world. We have to take it! Even more fortunately, there are now people like Marilyn leading the way, changing how money is taught to young people, which, as she explains in *Smarter Richer Braver*, is absolutely vital for their future success.'

— **Michael Gilmore**, author of *Happy Ever After* and founder of The Money Awareness and Inclusion Awards

'This is a so-much-needed book. In our fast-changing and evermore consumption-driven world, it is existential for kids and teenagers to learn about money, finances and investment at an early age. *Smarter Richer Braver* sets the foundation for that by providing essential guidance in a concise and easy-to-follow manner to parents and teachers.'

— **Sascha Janzen**, founder of Janzen & Co. and host of The True Wealth Project Podcast

'As a teenager growing up in the 1990s there was little information available to me around the important stuff...wealth, relationships, happiness and health. The part in *Smarter Richer Braver* that cut to my core was where Marilyn talks about school not teaching financial literacy in addition to parents not talking about it. I could certainly have done with your amazing book in 1990, Marilyn. But I'll happily settle for what you've shared in *Smarter Richer Braver*. A legacy and a journey that I'll be proud to share with my daughters so they are infinitely more financially literate than I ever will be. Thank you for being passionate enough to put your knowledge into *Smarter Richer Braver* for them.'

— **Robin Waite**, founder of Fearless Business and author of *Take Your Shot*

SMARTER
RICHER
BRAVER

SMARTER RICHER BRAVER

Unleash the power of
financial education and
turbocharge your teen's future

Marilyn L. Pinto

Rethink

First published in Great Britain in 2022 by Rethink Press
(www.rethinkpress.com)

For Yatin

And for parents everywhere who refuse to have their eyes wide shut anymore

Contents

Introduction

I'd like you to imagine that you are fifteen again, and everything is exactly the way it was then. You live in the same house, you go to the same school, you even hang out with the same bunch of friends.

Nothing's changed. Except for one thing: You are now financially empowered. You have a healthy money mindset and you know and understand how money works. You know how to make smart money decisions and how to avoid making stupid ones. You know the importance of saving, spending wisely and, most importantly, of investing early.

Knowing all this and feeling financially empowered makes you think, act and behave in ways that are consistent with building wealth and a financially secure future. All this at fifteen!

I'd like you to think about what a difference this would have made to the financial trajectory of your life. Don't stop there. Think further about how this feeling of financial empowerment would affect every other aspect of your life – your choice of career, your relationships, the risks you could take, the goals you could pursue and your general health and mental wellbeing.

If you're like most people on the planet, thinking about this is going to make you cringe and feel a keen sense of loss for what could've been. I know I certainly felt that.

I want you to imagine giving this gift of financial empowerment to your teenager, knowing it will be one of the most valuable skills they can acquire at this age – a skill that will help them step up, stand out and live a life on their own terms.

I can help. I'm the founder of KFI GLOBAL, an education company that specialises in financial empowerment programmes for teenagers. Thanks to KFI GLOBAL, over 5,500 teenagers now make smarter money decisions and are setting themselves up for a financially secure future. I've partnered with some of the biggest and most respected organisations in the region and have been regularly quoted in the national press on the subject of financial education and teens.

I didn't start this company because I noticed a gap in the market, I started it because I noticed a gap (more like a deep gaping hole) in my then eight- and ten-year-old daughters' understanding of money. While they were both academically smart, they were clueless about money, and this problem wasn't specific to them. Everybody else's kids seemed to have the same issue.

I didn't intend to start a company, I just wanted to enrol my kids in a programme that taught them about money in a thoughtful, holistic and intelligent way. There wasn't one. I knew what I wanted, and every programme I looked into came up way short. That's how and why I started KFI. It's a labour of love, created not just for my kids but for any kid who'd like to be financially empowered.

If you're looking for an inspirational, feel-good book about parenting, put this down quickly because this isn't it.

If you're looking for a book that will give you three hot tips that will transform your teens into financial gurus, then again look away as this isn't it.

However, if you're looking for a book that has some hard truths and valuable insights about why our teens are so clueless about money, how important this skill is, the ways it will transform their thinking and lives, what to look for in a good financial education programme, the common mistakes to avoid and a blueprint of how to financially empower them while keeping your sanity, then this is exactly the book for you.

This advice isn't from an academic's desk or an investment banker's multiple monitors, it is battle-tested on the treacherous terrain of teen classrooms and family dining tables.

I'm a parent of teenagers, and I know that parenting a teenager is like no other experience. No article, book or 'teen expert' can adequately prepare you for what's in store – the roller coaster of emotions, the paralysing worry as they navigate the twisted corridors of the teenage years, and the overwhelming sense of feeling dated because you find it impossible to relate to anything they're saying, feeling or doing. It's not a journey any parent comes out of unscathed and it's sometimes tempting to leave well enough alone and hope for the best. It's tempting to have our eyes wide shut.

We cannot. We must not. Not in this instance, not when there's so much at stake, and not when our kids are so deeply impacted by what we do…or don't do. We have to realise that the steps we take today as parents to financially empower our teens will dramatically affect their lives. Small efforts that will undoubtedly reap invaluable benefits.

No one (other than our teenagers) has more to gain. We can rest easy, knowing that we have equipped them adequately with the skills they will need to navigate financial decisions intelligently. We can be proud, knowing our teenagers are part of Generation Wealth: a generation that aims to be financially secure; a generation that's taking charge of their future; a generation that wants to do better, not just for themselves but for humanity as a whole. Being financially empowered enables them to do that.

I'm on a mission to bring this life-changing education to more teens across the world because this will empower them to step up, stand out and live a life on their own terms. That's my promise – smarter richer braver teens – because that's exactly what the world needs.

This book will take you through the journey that you can then guide your teenagers on. My five-step blueprint will help you understand what it takes to financially empower teenagers. Each step deals with an important part of the process and together they are proven to work and deliver results, faster and better than you'd expect, leading you to:

- Recognise that the financial empowerment of your teenagers is your responsibility – a watershed moment.

- Feel empowered as a parent as your actions in this area can and will affect their lives for years to come.

- Understand why this skill is so critical and take action in ensuring your teens are properly equipped with it.

- Engage on this subject with your teenagers with tact and empathy.

- Know what mistakes to avoid with your teens to save you the time, money and effort of repairing the damage and paying for the inevitable fault.

- Know what to look for in a professional financial education programme and ensure your teens get the best guidance possible at this critical juncture.

This is the book I would've liked to read – that I needed to read – so I could guide my kids better. It's also a book I wish my parents had read, so they could've adequately equipped me for the inevitable financial quagmires life throws at us.

If I do my job well here, as a result of reading this book you will take action to ensure that your teenagers are set on the right path to financial empowerment, so that they can step up, play full out and live a life on their own terms; so you may worry less. It's what we owe our teenagers; it's what we owe ourselves. You will also become a tad smarter richer braver yourself – I know I did.

ONE

A Lack Of Financial Education

We find our teenagers in an unenviable situation where they are woefully unprepared to make any financial decisions. They are in double jeopardy because not only are they uneducated about money but they are also specifically targeted by businesses and marketing companies that then prey on their financial naivety.

In this first chapter, you'll discover the impact of that lack of financial education on our teenagers. You'll also find out what happens when the worst-case scenario occurs for our teenagers, what the likelihood is that your teenager isn't facing the downside of their investments, and who benefits from keeping teenagers illiterate about money. Let's start by looking into the problem more deeply.

Seek first to understand

It's in our nature to look for quick fixes, instant gratification and magic bullets. We hastily throw half-baked solutions at convoluted, insidious problems and are quick to fly the 'mission accomplished' banner high and proud. It makes us feel smart and decisive; it makes us look powerful and saviour-like; it also makes for great social media news bytes – short and superficial – just like our attention span is primed to be nowadays. Take a closer look and you will see that many times such hurried and cursory actions, without a thorough well-examined study, only serve to exacerbate the existing problem.

Take the issue of the lack of personal finance knowledge in youngsters today. An issue as convoluted and insidious as any, because of the huge toll it takes on their future and that of the economy. According to the National Financial Educators Council, in the US alone the cost of financial illiteracy was calculated at US$415 billion in 2020.

This particular problem didn't garner much attention previously, but the COVID-19 pandemic and the ensuing economic meltdown thrust it into the spotlight worldwide. A slew of solutions followed: money track-ing and budgeting apps, parent-controlled debit cards, online resources, self-help books, mandatory lectures and fin-ed programmes... the list goes on. All touting to expeditiously, effortlessly and – for a small fee – rid society of this menace forever and save the future gen-eration from the perils of bad money choices.

If it seems almost too good to be true, it is. Many of these organisations failed to study and understand the battlefield properly before rushing to market lofty claims and promises. They didn't pay attention to the needs and motivations of the teenagers they were pur-porting to help; they just swooped down and lectured them on responsible behaviour.

They ignored moulding the mindset of these young-sters, while jumping straight into budgeting formulae. They assumed that what worked for adults would automatically work for teens, forgetting that teens aren't mini-adults – their brains are wired in completely different ways.

They oversimplified and dumbed down the content, not understanding that nuance and complexity is inter-esting and engaging, not to mention a more realistic representation of the issues at hand. They believed that personal finance could be summarised in a few quick tips, not recognising that doing so undermined the very learning they were hoping to impart.

They fell prey to the myth that teens need to be entertained with short punchy videos, notwithstanding the fact that it is only deep and profound engagement that elicits true behaviour change. They completely overlooked the way the content was taught to the teenagers, grossly undervaluing the use of a tried-and-tested methodology to ensure that the content was delivered in the most effective way.

They delivered a 'McProgramme', identical irrespective of who it was being delivered to, not realising how crucially important it is to customise and personalise the content and learning experience to the learner. They, like much of the education system, focused on telling the youngsters *what* to think, instead of showing them *how* to think.

All this didn't dampen the profits or valuation of these organisations, it just failed to solve the underlying problem. It laid out the equivalent of an attractive plaster over a deep gash, and hoped for the best.

We cannot afford to delude ourselves into complacency. Our kids deserve better. We shouldn't be so quick to mortgage their future for a fleeting feeling of self-satisfaction. We need to stop with the quick fixes. We owe it to them to think deeper about the problem, to understand the prevailing issues better and to plan our offensive with more forethought and a heck of a lot more consideration. We have to resolve to deal with not just the symptoms but more importantly with the deep-rooted problem. For it is only by deeply under-standing a formidable problem that we can ever hope to properly overcome it.

Money, money everywhere and not a whit we learn

Money, in some shape or form, affects almost every aspect of our lives – from where we choose to study, the amount of debt we take on, the career path we follow and for how long we work to our health, our relationships, our choice of investments and even our retirement.

Yet we don't have a single class in our education system that teaches us about how money works and how we can make smarter financial decisions. It doesn't matter where in the world you are, what you studied or how much you paid for your education, the topic of money is conspicuous by its absence in most schools' curricu-lums. Just in case you're tempted to think things have changed with the new-fangled/innovative/cutting-edge education system of the twenty-first century – they haven't.

Even in the few countries where financial literacy is mandated by the government, its appearance on the curriculum is nominal. There is no testing for students and no proper resources or training given to the teach-ers, who understandably then either gloss over this crucial topic or resort to teaching it as a maths-based skill – which it is not.

Teens today are squarely in marketers' sights. With unrestricted access to social media, they are being served up advertisements that are deemed appropriate by the respective algorithm gods, who seem to know our teens better than we do and can identify – and often influence – what they want to buy next. On the one hand, we have marketing companies spending tens of thousands of dollars training their staff in how to sell, and on the other, our teens haven't had any training whatsoever in making smart buying decisions. How can this be deemed fair?

With easy 'democratised' access to day-trading plat-forms, teenagers are sucked into get-rich-quick schemes, while becoming dangerously addicted to the gambling-style interfaces and 'gamification' these platforms una-shamedly tout. Not only do teenagers misunderstand the core principles of investing, they fritter away pre-cious time and money dabbling in these speculative and high-risk activities. How can this be deemed legal?

Thanks to the economic repercussions of the COVID-19 pandemic, our teens are going to graduate into some of the most economically challenging times in modern history. They will do so with zero training in money. How can this be deemed reasonable?

In the last decade, the whole job paradigm has changed irreversibly, with the disappearance of the pension-secured job and the rise of the gig economy. Our teens will have to manage multiple jobs – maybe even multiple careers – with no safety net or government-assured assistance. With no knowledge or awareness about how money works and how they can make it work for them, our teens are woefully unprepared. While it may not be our legal responsibility, it is surely our ethical and moral responsibility to ensure that teenagers get the education and support they need just to deal intelligently with the financial aspect of their adult lives.

Not if ... but when

When we buy any kind of insurance, we do it to cover our bases in case something untoward happens. This might happen or it might not. We still buy the insurance because the possible downside is much greater if we don't.

Smart people are all about reducing the downside. They buy their car insurance, home insurance, health insurance or disability insurance while hoping that they never have to claim any of it.

What about the instances when it's not a question of a possibility but more an extremely likely, presumably definite probability? When it's not if ... but when? Take the following scenarios:

- **When your teen has to choose a credit card:** Do they choose a card based on an attractive design or which football team is splashed across the front? Do they know the right questions to ask? Do they focus more on the benefits and rewards offered by the card? Do they know to ask about the associated costs and fees? Do they – as so many teens do – see this as free money or do they understand how quickly debt compounds and snowballs?

- **When your teen takes out a car loan:** Do they – as many teens and young adults do – simply buy the most expensive car they can get a loan approved for? Or do they understand asset depreciation and the host of other aspects they need to consider before making a decision?

- **When your teen goes shopping:** Do they fall prey to every marketing gimmick and sales tactic? Or do they understand enough about buying behaviours, what triggers them and how to overcome cognitive biases around buying?

- **When your teen lends money to friends:** Do they do this without giving it a second thought or do they understand how this affects their relationships? Can they evaluate the basis upon which they should make these decisions?

- **When your teen considers taking out a student loan:** Do they see this as a hall pass to a few carefree years before they begin to take on life as a responsible earning adult? Or do they understand the cost, long-term impact and how this should impact their learning and earning capability?

- **When your teen is old enough to start investing:** Are they susceptible to ubiquitous get-rich-quick schemes being peddled by scam artists? Or do they have an intelligent understanding of how investing works, what to expect and how best to start?

- **When your teen gets their first pay cheque:** Is their first experience with their earnings going to be a bloody one-two jab followed by a knock-out punch? Or a beautifully choreographed dance where they know exactly how to plan and manage their finances smartly so that they are consistently and effortlessly building towards a secure financial future?

There is no downside to ensuring that teens and young adults are empowered to take control of their financial lives. Research continues to prove how it leads to better decision-making, heightened confidence and increased self-efficacy. When the statistical likelihood of these situations arising is all but guaranteed, how can we, in good conscience, fail to insure our teens against their devastating impact? Let's remember that it's not if... but when.

Of course, there is always someone who stands to benefit from keeping our teens illiterate about money.

Cui bono?

Cui bono is a classical Latin term for who stands to benefit. It expresses the view that crimes are often committed to benefit the perpetrators, especially financially. Let's take a minute to go down this rabbit hole and think about who benefits from kids and teens not understanding how money works and being unable to control their impulse purchases or delay gratification.

Who benefits from teens being unable to identify and stay away from predatory marketing tactics such as advertisements served up to them on their phones and tablets? When our teens spend mindlessly on the next new shiny thing, who benefits then?

What about when our teens grow up into adults who now splurge their own money on lavish brunches and dinners instead of carefully considering how they can save and invest this money. Who benefits then? Or they take on expensive debt just to buy the latest-model SUV or have expensive holidays or buy overpriced clothes and extravagant gifts?

Do you know who benefits from their lack of knowledge in how investing works and what returns they can reasonably expect? Or from our young adults believing that they can speculate their way to success? Or from not knowing the trademarks of a financial scam and being so clueless about money that they willingly offer themselves up as victims to any slick-tongued salesman peddling a get-rich-quick scheme? Cui bono? What do you think?

Financial illiteracy should be a crime – it greatly harms those afflicted. It has catastrophic consequences, not just on their finances but on every aspect of their lives from their self-confidence to their mental health. It is actively detrimental to their future success and happiness. Not only that, it adversely affects their families who often have to face the ramifications of their bad financial decisions.

Yet, according to Leora Klapper, Annamaria Lusardi and Peter van Oudheusden in *Financial Literacy Around the World,* only 33% of adults worldwide are financially literate. That's 3.5 billion adults globally who lack an understanding of basic financial concepts. That's not even taking into consideration kids and teens, who are now spending more money than any generation before them ever did at their age. When faced with such ignominy we need to know why this is allowed to happen and we must do everything we can to stop it.

Quit playing games with our teens

This is a cease-and-desist request to companies peddling all versions of get-rich-quick snake oil to our teens: Stop it, really.

- Stop telling eight- to thirteen-year-olds they can learn all about bitcoin and how to invest in it in half an hour or less. (Yes, that's the age group the company advertisement targeted.)

- Stop trying to teach twelve- to fifteen-year-olds to trade stocks on online platforms. Most of these kids don't know the basics of personal finance and have no clear understanding of savings, budgeting or emergency funds.

- Stop making teenagers believe they are 'investing' when they are in fact speculating.

- Stop touting your gamification strategies. This is just a way to lure kids into consistent participation on the platform and get them hooked.

- Stop talking about 'democratising investing'. This is just a gimmick to beguile younger and inexperienced customers.

- Stop telling teenagers that they can get rich quick and with little training, by learning to pick stocks and time the market. Most teenagers don't have even a rudimentary grasp of debt and interest owed, let alone risk assessment and diversification. Again, these key ideas aren't on the get-rich-quick curriculum.

These young 'customers' have no idea what 'margin calls', 'options' or 'leverage' even mean. They aren't emotionally or intellectually mature enough to with-stand the manipulative and predatory marketing tac-tics you use. They can't yet assess dangers and risk. Stop. Please.

12 June 2021 marks one year since the tragic suicide of twenty-year-old Alex Kearns, a student at the Univer-sity at Nebraska. He killed himself because he mistak-enly believed he lost US$750,000 in an options trade. Isn't this heart-breaking enough for the industry to put some checks and balances in place? And no, offering education resources to users to read at will doesn't cut it. In the note Alex left before he threw himself in front of a train, he admits he had no clue to what he was doing. Do you need a more jarring wake-up call?

We can't protect our kids from everything. They are going to get their knees skinned and elbows bruised when they learn to ride a bike or climb a tree. They will probably have to deal with the mean kids and class bullies at some time in their school lives. They will undoubtedly feel the tremendous pressure of entrance exams and A-Level results when they're ready for university. They will likely get their hearts broken somewhere along the way. Yet, we try.

We ensure our kids wear protective gear when engag-ing in any kind of sport. We're constantly on the look-out for the slightest signs of bullying and then come down like a ton of bricks on the offender. As for the en-trance exams and A-Levels, we throw the kitchen sink at this problem. Extra classes, tutoring and a trip to the slums of Nepal building huts, toilets or whatever else is deemed purposeful enough to warrant a mention on university applications, is thrown in for good measure. Not much we can do about possible heartbreaks, but that doesn't keep us from trying mightily (and failing magnificently) to manage their personal lives, as unobtrusively as possible.

Yet, we're collectively burying our heads in the sand about their future financial situation. It's a certainty that they will face financial decisions which they will be ill-equipped to handle. It is a given that they will be subjected to predatory marketing tactics. It is inevitable that they will not fully fathom the weight or repercussions of student debt and that they will encounter financial scams and fraud, given their ubiquity. It's inescapable that they will fall victim to all manner of influencers and marketers preying on their insecurities to peddle the flavour of the month.

Their ignorance about intelligent investing practices will not only make them susceptible to financial scams but it will rob them of years of compounding wealth. Their naivety around the power money holds will subjugate them to being slaves to it for most of their lives. Their financial fragility will jeopardise their long-term success. All of this adversely impacts their mental health and wellbeing, their family and relationships, and every aspect of their adult lives. It undermines their ability to step up, stand out and live a life on their own terms.

We, as parents, as educators and as a society, know this to be true because most of us have lived through some version of these scenarios. We have seen this happen time and again; if not directly to us then to the people around us. Yet, we continue to naively hope that if ignored, it will go away. Our feckless attempts as a society to educate our kids around money are a sad reflection of this. These attempts are woefully inadequate, arrogantly optimistic and hopelessly reckless.

The eloquence of blah blah blah

Greta Thunberg's speech at the 2021 Youth4Climate Summit was a masterclass in eloquence in calling out BS from world leaders for failing to act on climate change. It was a classic case of telling the emperor he wasn't wearing any clothes.

The 'blah blah blah' eloquently told world leaders that young people are fed up with their empty words and promises. It perfectly articulated the frustration the younger generation feels with grown-ups charged with making decisions that will adversely impact their futures. Thunberg's speech was an impassioned plea that we need to do better by our youngsters – not just on climate control but on a range of looming issues that will disproportionately affect young people.

These are issues of global import such as the regulation of social media sites that serve up harmful content and advertisements to teenagers that are proven to cause or worsen mental health issues for them. In the summary of Frances Haugen's testimony on the NPR website in October 2021, we now have proof for what we previously only suspected.

It's obvious that these companies cannot and will not self-regulate, so it's time to enforce regulation and oversight from entities such as the Center for Humane Technology, Accountable Tech and SumOfUs for the predatory marketing practices of day-trading platforms targeting youngsters. We don't want any more slapping of wrists or of meagre fines that are a drop in the oceanic profits of the industry behemoths.

The time for reckoning is close. We need to clean up our act and ensure we don't earn the distinction of being known as the generation who fiddled while the world burned.

Before we move on, let's stop a minute and talk about the F word. It's not what you're thinking; it's not even 'feminism'. The F word I'd like to focus on in this section is 'fair'. Because life, particularly for women, can be unfair. This section is especially for those of you who have daughters.

The F word

Women are socialised to believe that they are bad with money and that it's unfeminine to talk about money. They are often portrayed as shopaholics and commonly seen deferring to men when it comes to making money decisions. Across the world, women trail behind in financial literacy scores. Since financial literacy is the bedrock of financial empowerment, women then tend to be less financially empowered, which is a crying shame because we need it more. According to Tanya Somanader in 'Chart of the week: The persistent gender pay gap', women typically earn around 80 cents to the dollar (it's even less for racial minorities and women of colour).

That gender inequality starts at a young age. There are several studies that show that boys receive more pocket money than girls. More studies show that parents tend to talk more to their sons than their daughters about money and investing. Fair isn't a word that springs to mind here. This causes women to be on the disadvantageous end of the income gap alongside the investing gap. We get used to the narrative that investing 'is not for us', 'we don't know enough about it' and that we'd rather just 'leave it to the men'.

The Fidelity Investments' '2021 Women and Investing Study' shows that women outperform men when it comes to investing. They spend more time researching their investment choices and take on more appropriate levels of risk compared to men. Women are also less likely to be impulsive in their investment decisions and to hold investments for the long term, whereas men tend to trade more often and thus reduce their net returns.

It's time we take definitive steps to obliterate these well-worn narratives about women and money. It's only fair, not just because of the following reasons:

- Because women earn less than men, they need to be smarter with their money.

- Women spend less time in the active workforce due to pregnancy and childcare. As a consequence, women are less likely to be covered by pensions or receive workplace benefits.

- Women tend to live around five to seven years longer than men. Therefore, not only do they earn less, they do it over a shorter period of time and then have to make it last longer while having less of a safety net to fall back on.

How can this be fair? It's not. It's unfair, unkind and disingenuous. Tipping the scales in favour of one sex isn't playing fair. Just because it's been done for ages doesn't make it right or acceptable.

We know better now. We know how harmful it is for women to be financially disempowered. It affects every aspect of their lives, not to mention their mental health and confidence. One of the main reasons women stay in abusive relationships is because they lack the financial means to be self-reliant if they leave.

Conversely, being truly financially empowered does wonders for women. It builds their self-confidence and helps them make smarter decisions, not just with regard to money but to other aspects of their lives as well.

Let's commit to using the F word more often and ensure that our daughters get fair treatment at home and in the workplace. It's only fair.

STUDENT VOICE – ARYAAN

Aryaan had always been fascinated by the topic of money, especially since he started a small online business. He had tried to learn more about money by watching videos on YouTube, but he soon realised that the knowledge he gained from these was limited. He could see a credibility issue as they all inevitably tried to sell him some product or another. He found that he was reacting to buying messages, to influencer-led marketing and to the usual sales tactics.

Since completing the programme, Aryaan has become more mindful and conscious of how and what he spends his money on. He notices the difference when he compares himself to his friends and classmates who seem to have no such compunction and just spend mindlessly on things they don't need. At home too, he takes a much more active role in financial decisions. He feels that learning about money has made such a difference to his life.

Aryaan is now confident about his future and believes that his money skills give him a huge advantage over other kids his age. He has easily identified and steered clear of scams and is mindful of not making impulse purchases.

He wants to carve out a career in music and is already making money by creating music that he sells. He has invested in learning more and is better equipped for what he sees as something he's interested in making a career of.

Summary

Money affects everything we do in our lives and yet teenagers are not educated in school about financial matters. Due to their naivety and lack of financial knowledge, they are preyed upon by companies who benefit widely by marketing to them on their phones and on social media so that they made bad decisions that impact on them and their families. We are calling on these companies to stop their relentless targeting of our teenagers. Right now.

In the next chapter we delve further into how teenage financial education is so elusive, why parents aren't supporting it and how to talk money with teens.

TWO

Let's Talk About Money

In this chapter you will learn the three reasons why financial education is so elusive for teenagers. I will delve into why parents aren't getting in on the financial education game, even when the stakes are so high. You will also get essential pointers on how to talk to teens about money, a better understanding on why financial education isn't really about money and why there is no app that can realistically achieve this.

Why is financial literacy still elusive for teenagers?

We all know how important it is to learn about money. We realise that our teenagers will undoubtedly be better off with this skill. We even understand that wealth is an outcome of financial literacy. Why, then, is financial literacy still so elusive for our teenagers?

There are three main reasons:

1. **Most schools, including high schools, colleges and even business schools, don't teach it.** Economics and business studies classes don't count either, as they do not teach teens how to deal with their personal money. When schools do attempt to teach personal finance, they do it in a way that most students find mind-numbingly boring.

2. **Parents don't talk about it.** They haven't had formal training in this subject. They learned the hard way, through trial and error and by making expensive mistakes. For the most part, they are barely getting by themselves and they aren't sure they are the best people to advise their teens on this subject.

   When parents do attempt to teach their kids about money, they too are guilty of doing it in ways that teens find mind-numbingly boring (see the pattern here?). In addition, most parents also pass along their own money biases, which at best don't serve their kids and at worst are actively detrimental.

3. **It's an unconscious incompetence.** Teenagers don't know that they don't know about money. This is mainly because most teens are clueless

about the need to learn about how money works and don't know how critical this skill is for their future success and wellbeing. They are only focused on getting good grades so that they can get into good universities and end up with decent jobs that pay well, but they are clueless about how to manage that pay cheque intelligently.

They don't realise that they will be tested on this skill every day of their adult lives and how they fare will colour every aspect, from the kind of job they choose to how long they will have to work, their relationships and their health. They don't understand that being financially literate directly impacts their ability to step up, stand out and live a life on their own terms.

The good news is that none of these problems are insurmountable. They are, in fact, ridiculously easy to overcome, especially if we act together. The majority of teenagers would like to learn about money but they want to do it in a way that's simple, fun and relatable.

We all – parents, schools and even society at large – have a vested interest in making sure that teens are financially empowered. More than that, we have a responsibility to them because the alternative and its aftermath is decidedly disastrous.

Three reasons why we sit on the sidelines

Given our experiences with money, the mistakes we've made and what we wish we knew about money when we were younger, how is it that we parents aren't up in arms? How come we aren't calling for massive decisive action to fix what we must know is a ticking time bomb? Why are we content to sit on the sidelines and wait for this to play out? Especially when we know deep down that there isn't any good way this can turn out. There are three reasons.

1. It's in our blind spot

As parents we have a number of blind spots when it comes to our teenagers and their lack of knowhow when it comes to money has to be one of the biggest. We either don't perceive it to be a problem, or if we do we make light of it or proceed to brush it off as a phase that our teens will grow out of. We assume they will figure it out on their own. We consider making money mistakes almost a rite of passage, something that can't be helped, but because we don't recognise it as a problem, we can't begin to solve it. We remain passive even in the face of impending doom.

There is another related issue here, a psychological phenomenon called 'inattentional blindness' where we fail to notice something because we are so focused on another task. As a result of our singular focus, we miss

LET'S TALK ABOUT MONEY

out on important information that isn't related to that task. As parents of teenagers, we are so focused on their test scores and college entrance exams, we easily fall prey to this. We don't notice their lack of understanding of money and how it works. And again, we can't solve what we can't see.

2. We play fin-ed football

We don't take action to financially educate and empower our teens because we think this should be handled by schools and colleges. After all, they're teaching our teens everything else. Also, they would ostensibly be better and more effective at delivering this sort of knowledge than we parents would. With the high fees we pay for 'innovative' and 'state of the art' education, we feel sure that our teenagers are being taught all they need to know about money. We skilfully pass this responsibility on and rest easy.

The problem is that the education system is equally good at this game. It throws the responsibility off, citing a lack of time, funds and resources. Their time, they feel, is better spent preparing teens for college entrance exams and ticking the boxes on all the government-mandated subjects. Their funds aren't enough to cover teaching an extra subject that isn't part of the regular curriculum and isn't government mandated to boot. They also don't have teaching staff and operational resources to pull this off, they say. They see personal finance as being firmly in the parental teaching domain and make an adept throwback to the parents.

With all these fantastic passes and throws being executed by the two stakeholders who have the most impact on the teenagers, the teenagers end up losing. Because we parents continue to delude ourselves that this isn't our responsibility, we aren't making a move to play.

3. We're out of mental bandwidth

We parents have too much on our plates. Between keeping our teenagers alive, fed and out of trouble and dealing with the elusive work-life balance, we don't have much mental bandwidth left over for tending to teens' financial educational needs.

This leads to 'tunnelling', which psychologists Eldar Shafir and Sendhil Mullainathan write about in their excellent book, *Scarcity*. A scarcity of time makes us put off important but non-urgent things, like writing a will or talking to our teens about money. Shafir and Mullainathan write, 'Their costs are immediate, loom large, and are easy to defer, and their benefits fall outside the tunnel.'

There is a cost to getting our teens a financial education that we'd rather not think about and we can easily defer this because we don't see the immediate benefits. This makes it easier to undervalue and leave out.

Remember our blind spot? We're not absolutely convinced they need that education anyway. They seem to be doing just fine. Therefore, we wait to deal with this issue once we're done with all the other urgent stuff, but we never seem to run out of the urgent stuff. Suddenly our teens are now off to college, or have started their first job and we still haven't given them the crucial financial education they need.

These three reasons give us an insight into why we, as well-intentioned parents who want the best for our teenagers, sit on the sidelines when we should be the star players in the game.

Eyes wide shut

Given why we sit on the sidelines, nobody could blame us for giving up and leaving it to chance. It's perfectly understandable why as parents, we'd have our eyes wide shut. It's because the alternative is exhausting... and hard... and exhausting.

We ignore the harmful effects of a host of products or services that are marketed to our teens, whether it's Facebook, Instagram or the latest Buy Now Pay Later (BNPL) offering targeting this lucrative demographic. We hope our teens are mature enough to know what's good for them, smart enough to see through blatantly false advertising and brave enough to stand up to peer pressure and societal expectations.

Trouble is, they aren't. They aren't meant to be. Their brains aren't fully developed yet. They can't easily rein in their teenage tendencies of overdosing on dopamine. Expecting them to is a lesson in futility. They need us to put the guard rails up for a while longer.

That's hard when every societal influence is hell-bent on pushing them to the edge by appealing to their propensity for instant gratification. It's unthinkable that businesses would prey on their lack of maturity and understanding, or worse still actively home in on what they know is a teenager's Achilles' heel, but they do. With laser-sharp focus.

Shiny objects, expertly marketed by influencers, made 'affordable' by easy credit card instalments or better still the 'no interest' BNPL schemes, and these poor unsuspecting teenagers and young adults are well on their way to a life of soul-sucking debt that's ridiculously hard to unshackle. BNPL is attractively packaged as a better alternative to credit card debt, which youngsters know is bad, but they don't know enough to know that BNPL could be much worse, if they're not careful.

Youngsters aren't careful. Joseph Campellone and Raymond Kent Turley state in their article 'Understanding the teen brain' that teens' prefrontal cortexes, the part of their brains responsible for executive functions like planning and control, only fully mature at the age of twenty-five. Because of this, teens are more likely to engage in risky behaviours. This is exactly what these companies are betting on, which affects our teens' self-esteem and mental health.

This hurts to watch, so we don't. Having our eyes wide shut is much more appealing.

If you think it's about money

Financial education is not just about money. Money can't buy happiness, they say. Let's not burden teens with learning about money, they say. Teens need to focus on their grades and getting into good universities, we shouldn't fill their heads with ideas of riches and wealth prematurely, they say.

That's a load of crock, I say. If anyone thinks financial education is all about money, they've completely missed the point.

When a teenager carefully considers the cost of student loan debt instead of blindly taking it on – that's an effect of financial education.

When a teenager conscientiously pays their credit card bills, on time and in full, and avoids credit card debt like the plague – that's an effect of financial education.

When a teenager starts investing in low-cost index funds and slowly but consistently keeps at it so that they get a head start on wealth-building activity – that's an effect of financial education.

When that same teenager, as a young adult, can take on a lower-paying job with better learning opportunities and better chances of growth in the future, all because they can manage their money better – that's an effect of financial education.

When this adult wants to strike out on their own, they can. They aren't dependent on their parents, spouse or the government, because they've made smart money decisions and are now self-reliant – that's an effect of financial education.

If this adult wants to consider leaving their job to pivot their career or to start their own business, they have the confidence to do so, because they have a nest egg to fall back on. They don't have to be buffeted around by the economy, or a horrible boss or the current unemployment rate – that's an effect *of financial education.* I could go on...but you get the picture.

On the other hand, when adults live from pay cheque to pay cheque, get into soul-sucking credit card debt, work jobs they hate just to pay the bills, or work for decades without any savings or wealth-building activity – these are effects of a lack of financial education.

Money is a leading cause of stress, divorce and mental health issues. Therefore, when as a result, these adults then suffer from unimaginable worry, strained relationships and serious physical and mental health issues – these are effects of a lack of financial education.

When they are forced to stay in a physically and/or emotionally abusive relationship because they can't afford to walk out – that's an effect of a lack of financial education.

When they suffer crushing remorse because they can't afford to give their family the security and lifestyle they would have loved to – that's an effect of a lack of financial education.

When they dread retirement, because they know they can't possibly afford it – that's an effect of a lack of financial education. I could go on … but it's too painful.

Financial education is not about money, it's about freedom and security. It's about mental and physical wellbeing. It's about self-love and self-care. Why on earth would we begrudge our teenagers that?

Is there an app for that?

There seems to be an app for everything nowadays. From shopping and dating to pet grooming and fuel refills, you needn't get off the sofa anymore. Recently there has been a veritable explosion in the number of money apps and digital offerings trumpeting claims about teaching kids and teens good money behaviour. From budgeting and investing apps to digital debit cards, they proclaim to (choose the bullet point that resonates most with you):

- Financially empower kids

- Raise financially smart kids

- Teach kids money management and investing fundamentals with real money

- Teach kids to earn, save, spend and (wait for it) invest

Just download and hold your breath.

Sounds lovely, doesn't it? Three cheers for the fintech industry for tackling this monstrous issue. Can we all pack our collective bags and rest easy, knowing the financial future of the next generation is in safe hands?

Not so fast. Let's take a minute to look into what's at play here. These apps and digital offerings are great at their core purpose, which is facilitating the digital transfer of money from parents to kids, helping kids to spend that money both online and offline securely, while enabling parental tracking and controls.

That's it. They do not, magically or otherwise, turn an overspending, financially clueless kid into a money whizz, never mind a savvy investor. Teaching teens to spend money, even if they do track their spending diligently, isn't financial literacy. Financial literacy and teaching teens how to make smarter money decisions is a lot more nuanced than that. In an article entitled 'Why can we not perceive our own abilities?', Decision Labs say that this exacerbates the Dunning-Kruger effect, which is a cognitive bias in which people with low ability at a task tend to overestimate their skill. Subsequently, you have kids with limited or no understanding of how money works, who now overestimate their ability to make smart money decisions. Can you see how dangerous this can be?

These money apps do undoubtedly have value; but only if the users are already financially responsible and knowledgeable. Therein lies the rub. Sidestepping this crucial caveat isn't serving teenagers, or their parents. There is no easy fix. Parents and educators still need to get down into the trenches and carry out the time-consuming, highly complex, yet infinitely rewarding task of teaching kids and teens how to model good money behaviour and make smarter money decisions.

We need to take the time to change and mould their mindset around money. We need to talk to them, answer all their wonderful questions and help to clarify their thinking around money. We need to develop their competence around money through deep learning and regular guided discussions, and ensure that this then positively impacts their thinking and behaviour. There is, at the time of this writing, no app for that. Instead of an app, let's start talking about money to our teenagers.

Have you had the money talk yet?

A couple of years ago, I was invited to a school to talk to the Year 7 students about the importance of financial education. One girl said that she didn't think she needed to learn about money because she intended to marry a rich man. Inwardly, I went on a rant decrying the sappy Disney movies that put these delusions of 'being rescued by a knight' into the heads of our young and oh-so-impressionable kids. Outwardly, I just smiled and told her that's it's always smart to have a Plan B. Thankfully, by the end of the talk she had scrapped Plan A and was determined to learn as much about the topic of money as she could. She even campaigned to her teachers to get me to come back in a few months for a follow-on session.

I wish I could say that instances like these are rare, where kids don't feel the need to learn about money, but they aren't. In some schools, students think that their parents have enough money so that they don't need to worry or think about it too much. Some students think that they are so talented in either sport or music that they will be raking in the big bucks soon and so also don't need to be concerned about money.

It is shocking how little teens know about money, but we can't blame them. Most parents haven't had the money talk with their teens and no one can blame us. We aren't given a lesson plan so we're not entirely sure what to say or how best to go about teaching our teens good money-management skills.

We're also afraid that saying the wrong thing might send them careening into a life of financial despair. We haven't had much formal training on the subject ourselves. We mostly learned from trial and error, and by making expensive mistakes – none of which we'd like to elaborate to our teens.

Given all of the above, our reticence is understandable, though wholly ill-suited to the task at hand. We all know that financial ignorance is dangerous...and expensive, and yet we do not adequately prepare our teens to handle, manage or even think about money. No matter what their career choices, the one thing teens are going to have to deal with as adults is money. They will be tested on this skill every day of their adult lives.

How they fare will affect every aspect of their lives – what they do for work, how long they choose to work, their relationships, their health, when they retire, their ability to take on risk and, of course, their stress levels.

There is light at the end of this tunnel. Here are a few pointers that might help:

- **Start early:** As soon as they say 'I want' would be a good time to talk about how money works.

- **Don't lecture:** Teens switch off when we get into lecture mode, so don't. Instead use stories to illustrate a point.

- **Avoid the gender gap:** Research shows that parents are more likely to talk to their sons rather than their daughters about money and investing. Don't do that.

- **Share the responsibility:** The 5th Annual Parents, Kids & Money Survey by T. Rowe Price from 2013 shows that while teens are more likely to ask their mum about money matters, more often than not women play the 'ask your dad' card, thus signalling to their teenagers that money is a man's domain.

- **Don't flaunt bad money behaviour:** Teens may not always listen to what we say but they are always watching what we do, so as hard as it is, we must model what we preach.

We need to write a new narrative for our kids, one in which they are taught how to manage money smartly and responsibly, in which they have the skills and the resulting confidence to make smart financial decisions. Because if anyone thinks financial education is all about money, they've completely missed the point.

STUDENT VOICE – HOLLY

Holly didn't think twice about spending all the money she was given. Her mum needed Holly to be more mindful and learn about money because lecturing her about it wasn't working. Holly just rolled her eyes and sighed.

Holly first attended the KFI programme as a ten-year-old and then again when she was thirteen. She was always keen and excited to learn about money.

'Nobody talks about this stuff in school, so it was cool that we got to learn and discuss so much about money during the programme,' she says. 'It really made a difference to the way I think about money now. My friends don't have the same awareness and I sometimes find their money behaviour shocking.'

Holly is interested in cooking and baking. She now makes a bit of money by taking orders from friends and family. 'They get a friends and family discount. It feels good to be smart with money now,' she says with a twinkle in her eye and a broad smile.

Summary

In this chapter we've learned the reasons why financial literacy is unobtainable for teenagers: schools don't teach it, parents don't talk about it and teenagers don't know what they don't know about money. Instead of dealing with it, we keep our eyes wide shut because we don't have the time or energy to deal with it.

We may think money buys us happiness but, in fact, we know that the effect of not being financially literate leads to stress, strained relationships and serious physical and mental health issues for our teenagers.

We need to talk to our kids about money and in this chapter, you've learned key tips to get that conversation started. In the next chapter you will find out why this resonated so deeply with me.

THREE

Who Am I Not To Try?

This chapter is deeply personal. It takes you through my journey from 'Hmm, that's odd' to 'I can't allow this to go on.' It gets into my motivation for setting out on this crusade and all the reasons I should have stopped, but didn't.

The three Ms I wasn't prepared for

I spent my thirties being mad at a lot of people. This was because I was hit with the three Ms that nobody and nothing adequately prepared me for.

1. Marriage

I expected the road to getting married to be tough. Finding the 'right one', deciding to commit and finally taking the plunge to be together forever seemed so amorphous, with just your intuition and not much else to guide you how to do this well.

I was certain, though, that once done, the rest would be a piece of cake. My life would follow the 'happily-ever-after' theme, just like all those Disney movies and romance novels. All I had to do was smile and wait for my happily-ever-after story to begin.

I smiled expectantly and I waited...and waited. Then I got mad. Mad at the people writing those stupid fairy tales and romance novels and making those unrealistic romantic movies. Mad at other married people for making it look so easy. Mad at my husband for not playing along to my stupid 'happily-ever-after' fantasy.

Nobody warned me about the amount of work that went into a marriage. I had heard a tremendous amount about 'finding' the right one. Nobody counselled me about 'being' the right one. Or about the fact that sometimes in a fight you have to give in, even if you're right (and I was always right). Or that sometimes you just have to breathe and let things pass, even if you think your spouse is being an idiot.

Luckily, I got over this. I've been married sixteen years now and am happy around 74% of the time. I've been told that's a good average.

2. Motherhood

This is something else I was woefully unprepared for. I envisioned motherhood to be walking with my kids in sunflower fields, baking cupcakes and blowing bubbles. Nobody warned me about the endless cycle of worry, anxiety and guilt. About the fact that your body, heart and mind will never be the same, ever again. That just when you think you've got things under control, there will be a torrent of new, unexpected, potentially unsolvable problems that come cascading towards you at breakneck speed.

Again, I got mad. Mad at other mothers who made it look so easy. Mad at the media for only portraying mums who are perfectly put together, while whitewashing the darker side of motherhood like postpartum depression and the never-ending guilt that weighs you down like a ton of bricks. Mad at my kids for not being 'little bundles of joy' all the time.

I got over that. My kids are now thirteen and fifteen and are happy about 65% of the time. I'm told this is a pretty good average for teenagers.

3. Money

This is a tricky one. Unlike the other two Ms, it didn't hit me all at once. I had a comfortable life and I wasn't in any financial trouble to speak of. For a long time, I lived under the misconception that I was doing quite well in this regard.

Nobody told me about long-term thinking, about investing early and harnessing the power of compound interest. Nobody talked to me about taking control, planning smartly and building wealth early on. This is one skill that is completely life-changing and yet nobody was teaching it.

Realising that my kids weren't being told or taught any of this was a watershed moment for me. I was mad at the education system. I was mad at my parents and the generation before us for not realising what a gaping hole this was in our understanding of the world, and how big an impediment it was in our ability to truly live a life on our own terms. I was mad at myself for living under the 'everything's just fine' delusion for so long.

This time, I didn't just get mad. I got even. I read, researched and studied. I was appalled at how widespread ignorance of this crucial topic was. I was dismayed at how everyone seemed either complacent or complicit in furthering this ignorance. The few voices calling for change were drowned out by a cacophony of voices peddling get-rich-quick schemes that seemed so much more palatable than real change, which can often be messy and hard. There seemed to be a lot of half-hearted and short-sighted attempts to bring about change in this domain, but those petered out quickly due to a number of reasons, chief among them being a lack of proper understanding of the underlying problem and an unimaginative way of trying to fix it.

Just telling teens what to do made little difference if they didn't properly grasp how important this was and how this would drastically affect their lives. Many of the financial education programmes were deeply flawed too, at least with respect to garnering interest from teenagers. All of this was just the tip of the iceberg that we were heading towards at full steam.

This led me to start a company, KFI GLOBAL, which specialises in teaching teens and young adults all about how to handle money smartly and responsibly. We financially empower them so that they can step up, stand out and live a life on their own terms.

It's amazing to see the difference this knowledge has on their behaviour and mindset because they now know and understand how money works, and more importantly how they can make it work for them. I hope it will go a long way in ensuring that they don't spend as much time getting mad as I did.

Who am I to try?

For a long while I was stuck on the 'Who am I to try?' question. Who was I to question the education industrial complex and tell academics and tenured professors that what they aren't teaching our teens about money is severely handicapping their ability to live up to their full potential? Who was I to tell other parents that this is an issue that needs their immediate, undivided attention? Who was I to tell financial industry experts that what they do by helping people better manage their finances needs to happen earlier?

A potent mix of imposter syndrome, a lack of experience and confidence, a terrifying fear of failing and useful excuses about time, money, kids and life kept me at the pondering and self-debating stage for longer than I care to admit. I'm an introvert. I grew up with a pronounced stutter that effectively took any sort of public speaking off the table. The thought of giving a speech was enough to make me want to throw up. I hated being in the spotlight, which I understood would be a requirement here. I had young kids who needed me. My husband and I were already running a business together.

There seemed to be tons of people out there who were more qualified and experienced than me. People who already had a huge social media following, who were in the education or financial services industry and for whom, it seemed to me, it would be a short leap to embark on this crusade and make a success of it.

I had built a watertight case about the futility of going down this path. The twenty-four-carat excuses I had dreamt up for myself were unassailable. Nobody could blame me for ditching this idea. Except an annoying voice inside my head that refused to shut up: 'If they are so experienced and knowledgeable, why is this issue largely unaddressed in society?'

It took a while for me to get to the stage where I could ask myself 'Who am I not to try?' and have a reasonable answer. I hadn't had any sort of financial education growing up, so I keenly felt this lack of what I came to realise was an essential life skill. I had kids who I wanted to make sure were not going to follow in my footsteps and make ludicrous money mistakes, whether by commission or omission.

I was a quick study and had a knack of explaining complex concepts simply and memorably. I saw vividly that this issue had the potential to derail lives if not addressed early on. I certainly cared enough to spend every waking moment obsessing about the best way to approach this and effect lasting change. I realised that I didn't need to be in the spotlight, I just needed to shine the spotlight on this critical issue. I had kids who needed to see me stand up for what I believed in, and to strive for significance and impact, like I hoped they would someday. I had the unstinting support of my husband, who I call my delusional angel (that's someone who believes in you without any good reason). Tell me again, I asked my stubborn self: 'Who am I not to try?'

An idiot, an imposter and an iconoclast

I am all three. Undeniably, unapologetically and deliberately so, and that's made me a better educator.

An idiot

I am often the resident idiot in the room because I need the things I hear and learn to make sense. I need them to be uncomplicated and easy to understand. If the content doesn't fit these two criteria, I'm not afraid to ask repetitive questions until it does. I'm certainly not shy about being the idiot. I often find that when things are complicated, it's because either the person explaining it doesn't understand it fully themselves or is telling you that you're too stupid to understand, so please leave it to them – a huge red flag. I need to be able to break down the things I learn into easily digestible bits that are readily remembered and effortlessly recalled, because then I can explain it to a nine-year-old child.

I also need to see the relevance of what I'm hearing and learning or it doesn't interest me. I say this makes me a better educator because teens like learning in the same way that I do. Being an idiot also makes me stubborn because I don't know any better.

When people much smarter than me thought that I should focus on financial education for adults because that's an easier and more lucrative market, I didn't listen. I didn't want to get people out of financial conundrums, I wanted to make sure that these kids never got there in the first place.

When they said I should digitise all my content and switch solely to an asynchronous, pre-recorded delivery because that's more efficient and scalable, I didn't listen. I thought it was important for teens to interact with their facilitator in person and for the facilitator to build rapport and trusting relationships with the teens in their care.

When they said I should partner with financial institutions and let them market their products directly to the kids, I didn't listen. I thought that would be particularly distasteful, and I am intentional about not partnering with any financial entity that would require this.

All the above-mentioned points would unequivocally attest to me being an idiot, but there is immense value in being one. Everyone should try it sometime.

An imposter

I am not an academic. I do not hail from the hallowed halls of academia. For the longest time I demurred to them, thinking that they knew what was best for everyone, until I realised they don't – not for everyone, not in all circumstances and certainly not on all issues. While they may have the best intentions, this does not always translate into doing what's best for the student. While I initially felt like an imposter, when starting KFI GLOBAL I had looked long and hard into what was being taught around money, how it was being taught, and more importantly what was not being taught, and it didn't smell right.

I knew there had to be a better way. This was too critical an issue to leave to chance or experience, especially when I needed my own kids to acquire this skill soon. I couldn't risk sitting and waiting silently on the sidelines, and academia is famous for its glacial pace of change. I was intrigued by what the entrepreneur Naveen Jain said in his article for *Inc.*, 'Why you should always bet on dreamers, not experts': 'Your ignorance is what makes you the best person to disrupt the industry.'

This is true because being ignorant allows you to ask the questions the experts can't; you can think in ways the experts can't, because they are boxed in by their assumptions; you can break rules the experts won't ever dare to. People from within the industry tend to tweak incrementally. I knew that incremental change wasn't going to cut it. A radical makeover was in order. I was also enough of an outsider to have no stake in the way things had always been done. I could tell the emperor that he wasn't wearing any clothes.

I was sufficiently affected by imposter syndrome to ensure that I relentlessly questioned my thinking and my ideas. I read and studied incessantly because I was insecure about my competence and profoundly curious about what I didn't know. I wanted to ensure that I was thoroughly prepared and better informed than anyone who could question my credentials. As Adam Grant says in his latest book, *Think Again*, 'Humility is a crucial ingredient of the mind, and I made sure I was dosing up regularly.'

Being afflicted with imposter syndrome led me to underestimate my skill; but that was OK because it made me a more intent learner. It didn't douse my vision; it genuinely served to inflame it and it fuelled my motivation to do better, to think better and to be better.

That's why there is immense value in feeling like an imposter. Everyone should try it sometime.

An iconoclast

That's a fancy word for a rebel: someone who criticises cherished beliefs or institutions, of which I am guilty. Read on for some of the cherished beliefs I wish to obliterate:

- **Teenagers are moody, irritable and disengaged because of hormonal changes.** There is not much credible evidence to prove this. In most cases they are this way because of a lack of proper sleep and diet – both nutritional and psychological.

- **Grown-ups always know better.** No, most times we are flying by the seat of our pants and just hoping for the best. We have no clue how things are going to turn out.

- **Kids cannot be trusted.** They absolutely can. As John Holt says in his book *How Children Fail*, 'Nothing could be simpler, or more difficult. Difficult because to trust children we must first learn to trust ourselves, and most of us were taught as kids that we could not be trusted.'

- **Fear and coercion are the most effective ways to get kids to learn.** That's not just manifestly false, it's actively damaging our kids and turning them off learning forever.

- **Teaching kids about money will somehow ruin their innocence and make them materialistic.** No, getting kids and teens to understand how money works makes them appreciate it more, makes them more mindful about money decisions and ultimately makes them more successful.

I am an iconoclast because I now know better and I know our kids and teens deserve better. There is immense value in being an iconoclast. Everyone should try it sometime.

A rebel educator

If you ask most teenagers how they feel about school, you will get responses typically ranging from bored and disinterested to confused and frustrated. While many say it's fun and they love it, what they are commonly referring to is their social circle at school and the interaction that affords – not the actual learning. Pretty much no one says they enjoy the learning.

Seventeen years and a ton of money spent to improve their intellectual capabilities and their fondest memories are of hanging out with their BFF. Does anyone else see a cavernous hole here? Is this what learning and school is meant to be? We can't let it be that way.

Learning shouldn't leave teens feeling disinterested, disengaged and bored out of their minds. It shouldn't make them feel disempowered, with no agency over their own learning, or constitute a cruel and unusual punishment.

How else can we explain the stress, anxiety and pure dread teens feel when they are evaluated on what they've learned? Kids and teens are biologically predisposed to learning. It's a powerful survival instinct humans are born with and it needs to be nurtured as such. We need to rethink, reimagine and perhaps revolutionise the way we expect teens to learn.

We need them to know that their teenage years are when their brains are more powerful than at any other time in their lives. This is because their neuroplasticity is peaking, so it's easier, faster and so much more effective to learn things at this stage. This is when memories are easier to make and last longer compared to adult years. On the flip side, teenagers are also neurobiologically prone to boredom so the way in which they are exposed to new information makes a world of difference.

That's where the rebel educator comes in. I want the teens we teach to be intrinsically motivated – not by some grade they get on an exam but because they see the value and benefit in the learning. I want them to be deeply engaged, not compliant, because they enjoy and look forward to the interaction. I want them to be intensely curious because that's their nature.

It's our responsibility as educators to kindle this deep engagement and intense curiosity, to ensure that teens feel profoundly empowered by what they're learning and to inspire them to keep learning long after it isn't required by the education system. Because only then can they know what it truly means to learn.

It's more than that. We need to dismantle the framework of fear and coercion the education system thrives on, so teens stop seeing themselves through the lens of exam results, aptitude tests and Instagram filters and realise that they are each unique and incomparable.

We need to stop forcing teens into whatever metaphorical box is currently mandated by the powers that be and actively encourage them to own the wonderful traits that make them stand out. We need to understand that standardised tests cannot measure empathy, compassion and kindness – the main qualities of an evolved human being.

We should take time to see them as individual students, not just a class. We need to build trusting relationships with them to inspire them to a global consciousness, not just a nationalistic one; a sense of justice, not just lawfulness; and a respect for life – all life. It's what a rebel educator does and it's what I strive every day to do.

I have a dream…

I have a dream for a generation who aim to be financially secure, a generation who recognise money for what it is – a tool that affords them better life choices, which they need to learn to use and leverage. These young people don't want to be subject to the vagaries of the economy but know and develop their identity as valuable contributors to society.

I have a dream for a generation who refuse to be beholden to archaic rules and ideologies and see the need to discover new, fresh ways of thinking that can afford everyone a better quality of life. They will not be defined by their grades and test scores but by a vision, path and work they love.

I have a dream for a generation who want to be self-reliant and take charge of their own futures, refusing to follow the thoughtless, tired and toxic ways of the generations before them. They want to carve out a future that's fair and inclusive.

I have a dream for a generation who want to do better, not just for themselves but for humanity as a whole. This generation realise all humans are interconnected and we cannot truly progress or thrive at the expense of any.

This generation know that our best hope as a species is to work together to combat global challenges. They realise that being financially empowered enables them to step up, stand out and live a life on their own terms.

That's what I call Generation Wealth – a generation who are smarter richer braver. Because that's exactly what our world needs.

Forget passion, try obsession

I often get told that I'm passionate about what I do, but I disagree. Passion is too mild a term for the way I feel about the work I do. I'm obsessive. That's what enabled me to curate a programme and a methodology that has revolutionised the way financial education is taught to teenagers.

Being obsessive means I always want to do the right thing for the teens in my care. This has earned me the trust and gratitude of parents. I want them to get the chance to learn this critical life skill so that they don't repeat the mistakes of the past generation and be financially empowered so that they can take charge of their financial future.

I obsess daily about how to reach more teens so they can leverage this knowledge for a brighter future and whether I am doing enough to further this cause. This is why I keep pushing every day, even when the obstacles seem insurmountable, and this is why I enjoy the journey.

This obsession is why I smile through it all.

Summary

In this chapter you've learned about me and what has taken me on this journey to educate teens about money. I've given you an honest portrayal of the three Ms I wasn't prepared for – marriage, motherhood and money. I've given you an insight into the person I am, what drives me and how I have worked hard against allowing imposter syndrome to hold me back and prevent me achieving my goal.

Now that you understand me, you will understand why I am obsessive about what I do and the methodology I have created that has changed completely the way financial education is taught to teenagers. In the next chapter, we will take this a step further and you'll discover the importance of shaking up the status quo.

FOUR
Now Is The Time To Learn

H ere we talk about what happens if we don't step up to change the status quo around financial educa-tion, why it's hard work and how the lack of this skill is hampering our teens' success. We also look at the main benefits this skill offers our teens, while stressing that there's no better time to teach them than this. Let's start by looking at why bringing about a change in financial education is such a struggle.

The unsavoury alternative

There is real resistance to changing the status quo around financial education, or rather the lack of it. A lack of funds, resources, training and time are the causes most commonly cited. Yet none of these stand the test of reason. One just has to consider the alternative to realise that the cost of providing this education to teenagers is massively outweighed by the potential benefits.

More so than past generations, teens today are exposed to myriad earning and investing opportunities. Few are legitimate and most are highly dubious. From multi-level marketing schemes and stock and forex trading platforms to highly sophisticated investment instruments and financial scams, navigating young adulthood without being ensnared requires a keen sense of financial awareness and a BS-detector par excellence.

We cannot hope for or expect any self-regulation from the industries proffering these products to naive and gullible youngsters. What should be considered outrageous and indefensible is sadly business as usual. To make a bad situation even more appalling, social media influencers are now getting in on the game and weighing in on what they consider to be 'a good investment'. Never mind that their recommendations are plainly paid advertisements. Never mind that they have little-to-no actual knowledge about what they are so glibly endorsing. Never mind that most times their recommendations are clearly antithetical to sound investing and long-term wealth building.

The grown-ups in the room are either oblivious to these dangers or are vehemently defending the 'lack of funds, time and resources' rationalisation. Meanwhile

NOW IS THE TIME TO LEARN

the youngsters are following the entrancing music of the Pied Piper leading them off the cliff.

We can stop our teenagers from getting into sticky money situations or falling off the financial cliff more easily than we thought, simply by working upstream.

Upstream work

In his book *Upstream*, the *New York Times* bestselling author Dan Heath reflects on a public health parable where you and a friend are picnicking by a river and hear a shout coming from the water, as a child is drowning. Instinctively you both jump in to save the child, but you then hear another, and so dive in again to the rescue, followed by another, and another and so on. As you continue to rescue the drowning children, your friend wades out of the water, leaving you behind. '"Where are you going?" you demand. Your friend answers, "I'm going upstream to tackle the guy who's throwing all these kids in the water."'

This parable exemplifies our task in teaching teenagers how to handle money smartly and responsibly. We have to work upstream, where we can educate them about money, instil rational money behaviour and ensure that they develop a healthy mindset around it.

The problem is, as Dan Heath so eloquently says in *Upstream*, 'upstream work is hard'. It requires us to plan and prevent rather than react and rescue. There is so much more excitement with the rescue, whereas the prevention bit seems non-newsworthy in comparison. After all, who wants to hear about stuff that didn't happen when it's more thrilling to hear about saving people on the brink of bankruptcy?

Upstream work, Heath says, is also 'slow and maddeningly ambiguous, compared to downstream work which is fast and tangible'. Financially empowering teenagers is clearly upstream work. It takes time and effort to instil sound money principles, and its effects aren't always immediately obvious and are often hard to tabulate in the short term.

Simply giving teens financial knowledge is ineffective. We need to take into account changing their attitudes and mindset. We need to pre-empt their resistance to change, while ensuring that they are able to absorb the learnings and then implement this in their everyday lives, so that they feel truly empowered to make smart financial decisions.

This takes time and intentional effort, both on the part of the parents and the teens involved. In a world that promotes and glorifies instant gratification, this isn't easy, but it's the only way that works well and for the long term.

That's the kind of change we need for our teenagers. Not fleeting and momentarily inspirational but deep-rooted and life-changing. Success will come, quietly but powerfully, and will reflect not only on our teens' financial lives but in every aspect of their lives, from their relationships and career choices to their mental health and wellbeing. That's how inextricably linked this issue is in their lives.

Therefore, even though preparing our teens to handle money is hard, we need to commit to it. Bringing about systemic change is always difficult, but it's intensely worthwhile. That's exactly why it demands our tenacity and undivided attention.

Only by doing this and giving our teenagers the financial education they deserve will they have the competence and resulting self-confidence to make smart financial decisions.

Release the handbrake

If I asked you to close your eyes and envision the kind of life you'd like your teenager to have as an adult, you'd probably think of something like this: You'd like them to be happy, working at a job they love and care about, have a great work-life balance and spend quality time with their families. You'd like them to be able to afford a great quality of life and be able to help their family out in times of need. I'm sure you'd also like them to be self-reliant, financially secure and feel a deep sense of fulfilment in their lives.

Think about the lives of many people around you who are stressed and anxious, working jobs they hate for bosses they despise, just to pay the bills. They live in fear of losing their jobs, have hardly any savings to fall back on, no financial safety net and lots of debt to top it off. They are terrified of retirement because they know they can't afford it.

Can you see the yawning gap between these two scenarios? Can you see that the way people think about and manage money makes them financially empowered?

Yet as we have seen, this isn't something our teens instinctively learn (unlike how to argue and roll their eyes) and they aren't taught this in the current education system either. They grow up thinking that all their money problems will be solved once they get a job, not realising that the ability to manage a pay cheque intelligently is a skill most of them haven't been taught.

Most parents also are quick to support part-time job opportunities, even for younger teens, thinking that this will teach them time management, prioritisation and interpersonal skills, while also showing them the value of money and getting them to make smarter money decisions. While the first three might be true, I very much doubt the effectiveness of having a job on the latter two. We parents shouldn't be so quick to make the leap of logic that giving teens an opportunity to work and earn will ensure that they are more mindful about money and will make smarter money decisions.

I started working at twenty-one and it took a decade and a half before I had cultivated the right financial mindset, gained the knowledge and then modified my behaviour to reflect this. I wish I was the exception; sadly I was the norm. Things haven't changed much since then either.

Teens today spend more money than any generation before them but grow up without any financial education whatsoever. Earning more money without being financially educated just means spending more money in the same ways they're used to. Societies everywhere are teeming with examples of grown-ups doing this. Why should we think it will be any different with the teens?

Also, many countries around the world have regulations in place that allow teens to work, but there is no correlation to these teens being more financially savvy as a result.

We need to be intentional in teaching teens about money. This isn't something they are likely to figure out on their own. They might, but it will cost them heavily in terms of time, money and self-confidence. This lack of confidence, according to a research project by Principal Financial Group and renowned behavioural economist Dan Goldstein in their article entitled 'We make 35,000 decisions per day, but 7 in 10 postpone major financial decisions', is the primary reason many grown-ups put off making major financial decisions. It's not the lack of money, as was previously assumed, it's lack of the right, confident mindset that being financially educated affords. They commonly put off saving, investing and retirement planning, for example, which has long-term detrimental effects on their financial wellbeing.

It's like driving with the handbrake on. It will hamper their success, slow down their career growth and restrict their wealth-building endeavours. Being financially educated enables them to overcome these obstacles because they will then have the competence and resulting self-confidence to make smart financial decisions.

It's time to release the handbrake.

The effect of financial education

How does financially educating our teenagers help them? Let's delve into the top three ways:

1. It moulds their mindset for financial success

This is probably the most momentous change that happens. Sonya Mann from Inc.com quotes bestselling author and coach Tony Robbins in her article entitled 'Tony Robbins says success is only 20% skill – and the rest is all in your head', saying that success is achieved through a plan that is 80% psychological and 20%

strategic. That's why it's so important to focus on the psychological aspect first. You have to work on getting their mindset right to remove limiting beliefs and negative associations towards money. I always find it surprising how prevalent this is in teenagers.

Many teens I've taught think that it's not necessary or important to learn how to handle money smartly. They see rich people as cheats, rogues and manipulators; they view money as a necessary evil where they only need to have 'enough to meet their needs' and are convinced that being wealthy is accompanied by inevitable stress, anxiety and a loss of morality.

Many adults, too, seem to constantly vilify 'rich people', who they see as selfish, power hungry and devious. They believe they take undue advantage of and manipulate unsuspecting 'poor people', who they see as the good guys.

It's no wonder, then, that so many teenagers develop a mindset of money aversion or avoidance. It's imperative that we talk through this and help them to see that this does not serve them.

Once they begin to change their attitude, their interest and motivation levels in learning about money shoot up and they become more purposeful, committed and engaged, which of course helps them to learn better. This mindset is also extremely beneficial in other ways because it makes them become more aware of unhelpful media influences and begins to push back against common stereotypes.

More importantly, it trains their reticular activation system (RAS) – the programme in our brains that filters information as it enters, only allowing in information that aligns with our thoughts and beliefs. If you've ever thought of buying a car, and then proceeded to see that brand of car everywhere, this is the RAS working.

It works in the same way for money. With their new mindset, these teens now notice when people talk about money and how people spend money, and are more attentive to money-related issues. They become more aware, careful and mindful of money as a whole and are much more likely to recognise opportunities to earn and make money. This plays a huge role in their eventual financial success.

2. It gives them a head start in building and growing their wealth

Once teens learn the basics of smart money management, they can then be introduced to the 'pièce de résistance' of financial education – investing! Learning about and then implementing these lessons will give them a massive advantage over everyone else, who typically won't learn how to invest intelligently until much later, if at all, thus losing out on the scarcest resource of all – time.

Time is something that adults don't have. Teens can use this time to harness the power of compound interest, which according to Albert Einstein, is the most powerful force in the universe.

A 2021 article on Bloomberg.com entitled 'Warren Buffett becomes sixth member of $100 billion club', states that the billionaire businessman and philanthropist is one of the most successful investors of all time, in the main because he's used compound interest to his advantage. He started investing at the age of ten and has kept at it for the last eighty-one years and counting. That's his secret – time. It's not just his investing acumen but the fact that he's been a phenomenal investor for so much longer than most people. Buffetts' current net worth is over US$99 billion; US$70 billion of which he accumulated in his mid-sixties.

Statistically most grown-ups start investing in their late thirties or early forties. That's when their career growth is escalating and there's a bit more money in the bank for them to consider investing, but they have lost out on almost two decades of compounding growth because they started so late. This is definitely not something we want our teens to emulate. Getting teens to understand and act on this is invaluable. Instilling these habits early on through solid financial education gives them a head start in their wealth-building activity.

3. It elevates their understanding of life

The Rosetta Stone is a famous engraved stone from 196 BC Egypt. When the Rosetta Stone was discovered, nobody knew how to read ancient Egyptian hieroglyphs. Because the inscriptions on the stone said the same thing in three different scripts (hieroglyphs, demotic and Ancient Greek), and scholars could read Ancient Greek, it become a valuable key to deciphering the hieroglyphs.

Financial education works a bit like the Rosetta Stone. Before teens gain this important knowledge, they tend to view life through the myopic lens of grades and college acceptance. They blindly follow the herd in well-worn academic and career paths, not stopping to question whether there are other more interesting but less commonly opted for alternatives. Alternatives that could be better suited to their unique talents and interests. They also tend to take parental financial support for granted and are dependent on it for longer.

Once teens learn and understand how money works, how to use it wisely and how they can get their money to work for them, they begin to see and make sense of other aspects of their lives using this new useful lens. They realise what it means and more importantly what it takes to be independent and self-reliant.

A lot of teens want to be entrepreneurs, and having a good financial education gives them a deeper insight into what makes a successful one. Being financially educated helps them to evaluate different academic and career options based on their life goals and vision. It enables them to have a broader, more holistic view, while understanding what it takes to achieve that.

These three remarkable effects of financial education on teenagers are testament to the value of this critical knowledge. Each one on its own is powerful enough, but together they act synergistically to boost the impact manifold. You have to get in there now to start their financial education.

Why now's the time

To understand why the teenage years are the best time to financially educate our children, it is crucial that we understand something of teenage brains and how they think.

Until recently, it was thought that the teen brain was similar to the adult brain, just newer. This apparently is far from the truth. In their seminal book, *The Teenage Brain*, authors Frances Jensen and Amy Ellis Nutt state that 'teen brains are both more powerful and more vulnerable than at virtually any other time in their lives. Due to heightened brain neuroplasticity, they learn faster at this stage.' They go on to explain that the knowledge becomes more entrenched the greater number of times information is repeated, which strengthens the neural connections.

That's why it makes sense to teach teens about handling money smartly at this stage because the knowledge gets hardwired in them more quickly and effectively than in adults. With a little reinforcement, this critical knowledge gets cemented and their altered behaviour now becomes instinctive.

It becomes an 'unconscious competence'. They get so good at it they don't even realise they are using that skill because it becomes second nature to them. They are instinctively more mindful about spending money because they are intentional about thinking about it. They are better equipped to prioritise their needs over their wants.

Indeed, they are better at distinguishing between the two and better trained to resist impulse buys. Delayed gratification and impulse control are the cornerstones of what it means to be financially educated. These abilities have ramifications beyond just the financial realm. They correlate to better academic performance, higher paying jobs, better health and more successful relationships.

Another reason to teach teens these skills is so that they can see beyond the façade of slick sales techniques and glossy, glamorous advertising messages. Teens are vulnerable to the power of suggestion. With unrestricted access to the internet and social media, they are inundated with suggestions at the touch of a smartphone. They aren't trained to evaluate these suggestions or advertisements. Getting teens to then think critically about what they see and what is offered becomes imperative to their physical and mental wellbeing.

A key part of financial education is being taught how to critically evaluate advertising messages, to be able to question their veracity and develop a healthy scepticism about the claims they make. This particular training and skill development has far-reaching consequences in so many aspects of their lives.

Another key consideration with regard to teen brains is the fact that the human brain develops from back to front. This means that the prefrontal cortex isn't fully functional until their early twenties. The prefrontal cortex is the area of the brain responsible for insight, risk assessment, judgement and planning. Little wonder then that our teens seem so lacking in these areas and a clarion call to why we still need to keep the guard rails up with regard to setting limits and restrictions with our teens.

In the book, Jensen goes on to say that while teen brains are 'primed to learn, they are also exceedingly vulnerable to learning the wrong things. This means that a little bit of stimulation to a teenage brain, can lead to a craving for more stimulation that can, in certain situations, result in a kind of overlearning – commonly known as addiction.' She says that teenagers get addicted to every substance faster than adults, and once addicted have much greater difficulty ridding themselves of the habit. This is worrying on all counts, especially with the startling rise of tobacco, drug and alcohol abuse among teenagers.

There might be one more addiction that's far more insidious, mainly because it's wrapped up in the cloak of respectability and professionalism. That is online trading platforms that lure unsuspecting teenagers. It's easy to see the irresistible appeal these platforms have for teens:

- They all leverage technology in innovative ways, which is always a hit with the present technophile generation.

- They offer a constant stream of dopamine hits with notifications and messages.

- They offer beguiling promises of quick financial wins and 'investor' status.

This is aside from the user interface being attractive and frictionless – all the better to entrap teens with; the warnings and disclaimers being glossed over – all the better to confuse them with; and the 'gamification' of the platform – all the better to keep them addicted.

It's key to remember here that behavioural addictions are just as dangerous as chemical addictions because they make use of the same brain circuits and so deserve just as much oversight. Depending on industry self-regulation here is akin to the fox guarding the chicken coop. It's unreasonable and just plain unworkable due to conflicts of interest.

It's up to us as parents to step in now to ensure our teens don't get ensnared. They are inadequately equipped and thus dangerously vulnerable to the dangers lurking behind the innocuous screens. We cannot afford to wait as there is too much of a downside. We are the first line of defence for our teenagers and the time to act is now.

Catch 'em young

Frances Jensen and Amy Ellis Nutt write in *The Teenage Brain*, 'the types of cues and stimuli that are present during brain development change the way the brain works later in life.' Marketing companies use this to their advantage. That's the whole point of the billions of dollars of advertising targeted at kids and teens. They know that if they catch them young, they've got them for life. Just the junk food marketing to kids and teens is a US$2 billion a year industry. Considering the life-long impact of these influences, such as obesity or other health problems, we parents should be mindful about the cues and stimuli our teens' brains are being subject to.

Teaching kids and teens this early on will ensure that:

- Their brains are trained to respond in the right way to financial cues.

- They instinctively make the right financial choices.

- They get a head start on their wealth-building activity as they are able to harness the power of compound interest.

Teens find the topic of money fascinating, and if we parents don't take the lead in introducing them to this the right way, they run the risk of being unduly influenced by their friends, social media and marketing companies peddling all manner of financial products, irrespective of whether or not they are in the teens' best interest.

That's the nature of the beast, it's just business for these entities. It isn't for us as parents of these teens. It's personal.

We should care deeply about what influences their mindset and behaviour around money. We should care deeply about the effect these targeted ads have on our teens. We should care deeply enough to ensure we set the stage for our teens' introduction to money and all money-related matters.

We are uniquely positioned to ensure this happens, and while I'm not suggesting this is easy or convenient, it is a responsibility we cannot shy away from. Because if we do, we can be sure someone else will step in and there's no accounting for their agenda or interest.

STUDENT VOICE – TRICIA

Tricia was a twenty-one-year-old business management undergraduate, and though she had a ton of finance-related classes, not a single one of them related to personal finance. 'Just loads of formulae and definitions that seemed pointless and irrelevant. We learned about kinds of stocks and debentures but I struggled to understand it all and how we would actually use any of it,' she said.

By her own admission, Tricia was clueless about money. 'I saved until I had accumulated enough and then spent it all mindlessly, and the cycle just continued. I used to win money because of the dance competitions I participated in and in a couple of days would burn through it all. I had no idea how to budget my allowance and I was often broke, with no money left over for food or transport.'

On completing the KFI programme, Tricia said it had changed her entire outlook on money. 'I developed a positive mindset about money, became more aware of my choices and that changed my behaviour. My money choices are now so much more considered and it's made me so much wiser.' She goes on to say, 'I intend to start investing now that I understand so much more about the subject and feel confident enough to take the first steps.'

Summary

This chapter covered the impact of not challenging the lack of financial education for our teens and how it holds them back from achieving success in life. The three ways financial education positively impacts our teenagers are by:

- Moulding their mindset for financial success

- Giving them a head start on growing their wealth

- Elevating their understanding of life.

We've also learned about how a teen's brain works and why that means we have to start early to address this gap in their education.

In the next chapter we will expand on this to look at why teens need to be encouraged to think outside the box to bring out the rebel inside.

FIVE
Think Outside The Box

This chapter focuses on why teens need to be encouraged to think outside the box and bring out that rebel in them. We also investigate 'finfluencers' and the impact they have on our teenagers, and look at the use of technology within this arena.

Rebel thinking

Rebel thinking is the ability to think independently, not to be boxed in by existing frames or swept up by the common narrative. Teenagers need to be able to critically evaluate information they come across. As crucial as rebel thinking is, it's not a skill that's actively cultivated or encouraged in teenagers. We are more concerned with getting them to follow rules and directions than encouraging them to question the value and utility of said rules. We would rather make sure they fit into metaphorical standardised boxes, shaped by the education industry, than allow them to embrace and explore their wonderful individuality.

We focus more on them following a predetermined, well-trodden path, rather than the possibility of them forging a new, self-determined one. However, we parents feel that the stakes of non-conformism are too high. We don't want our teens to be a casualty of the unaccepting system.

Let's consider the upside for a moment. Now, more than ever – with the explosion of the 'influencer' culture and the powerful algorithms curating our social media feeds – teenagers need to exercise the power of rebel thinking. Being financially aware and astute demands that they hone their BS radar. While being knowledgeable about money helps, the ability to question existing paradigms and imagine new ones is a key strength.

Only then can they see though the predatory marketing tactics that are specifically targeted at them. Then they can question the dubious financial advice that's undoubtedly targeted at youngsters, precisely because they are mostly ill-informed.

Rebel thinking will help teens carve out their own identity instead of blindly identifying with someone based on trivial issues. It will protect them from being unduly influenced by nefarious entities and help them develop a sense of confidence in their ability to think through problems on their own, instead of instinctively running for help at the drop of a hat. Important to this rebel thinking ability is the subtle vote of confidence we, as parents and educators, give them in our daily interaction with them to show that we:

- Trust them to make good judgements

- Count on them to do the right thing

- Believe they can and will make valuable contributions to the betterment of humanity.

We need to encourage our teens to think differently. Teens today also have a finely developed sense of fairness and global consciousness that's essential to rebel thinking. We just need to trust them to get on with it and be willing to challenge authority and established ways of thinking. We need them to break out of existing norms that no longer serve any justifiable purpose and to rebel against social injustices and repression. Their ability to employ rebel thinking intentionally and consistently is a pivotal factor in their ability to live braver lives.

All that glitters

The explosion of self-help books on personal finance is testament to the demand for advice in this realm. We need to be wary of what and who we listen to, because when it comes to telling you what to do with your money and why you aren't rich yet, it's easy to drown in the cacophony of advice that passes for financial wisdom.

In her critically acclaimed book *Pound Foolish*, Helaine Olen writes: 'These experts paint themselves as our financial saviours, while often neglecting to mention they make a living (and a good living) not just from their television appearances and books but by their agreements with everyone and everything from mutual fund companies and credit reporting agencies – not to mention the host of "products" they try to sell us. This sets up a basic conflict.'

Olen's book gives readers a scathing commentary on popular personal finance experts of our time, from Suze Orman and Robert Kiyosaki to Dave Ramsey and David Bach, most of whom earned their money by convincing many of us that we are so helpless that we need the help of their books and product lines.

Olen also tells of Harvey Houtkin, the father of day trading, who made his millions not from convincing others that they had the ability to make successful stock picks themselves, but by racking up millions in commissions from customers of his day-trading firm while losing hundreds of thousands of dollars on his own investments.

It's important for us to teach our teens how to critically evaluate the advice or advertisements they come across, particularly because the advertisements for all manner of money-making or investing schemes are increasingly targeted at older teens. Whether it's day trading or crypto currency investing, 'finfluencers' are now all the rage, feeding our teens the slick, snappy thirty-second video reels that claim to demystify investing and show them how to make hundreds of thousands of dollars with little investment of time and just a bit more in terms of money.

Many of these influencers are paid by companies to promote certain financial products, many of which they hardly understand or invest in themselves. These 'finfluencers' are not licensed or regulated, which in turn means no accountability.

Many teens jump headlong into these schemes but haven't heard of 'due diligence'. That's why a key part of financial education and empowerment programmes should delve deeply into financial fraud and scams. Teens need to know what financial scams look like and why so many people fall prey to them. They need to know the common terms and phrases scammers use and understand what 'due diligence' means, why it's important and how they can do it themselves. They need to be shown how widespread financial scams are, and the devastating impact they have on the lives of those affected. This makes it real for them.

They start to see how scammers prey on people's financial naivety and begin to understand why so much financial fraud goes unreported, due to shame and guilt. Most importantly they are able to protect themselves and others around them because of this knowledge and understanding. They also apply this learning in other areas of their lives, like seeing through fake promises and claims made by many advertising companies.

The ability to keep a calm head and realise that all that glitters is not gold is a critical life skill. That's such a crucial part of an effective financial empowerment process.

The fault in our stars

If the powers that be had a diabolical plan to keep much of the world's population subservient, stressed and short-sighted because that suited their business interests, all they would have to do is deliberately ensure that much of the world's population is unschooled in the subject of money. Their plan is working swimmingly.

Calls for change to the financial literacy situation have largely fallen on deaf ears or been rewarded with half-hearted attempts that fizzle out due to a lack of con-tinued interest or funding. It makes perfect sense that there is a lack of interest from these powers that be – they are, after all, safeguarding their golden goose. It would be silly of them to school their customers in the subject of money when it is precisely that ignorance that they are profiting from.

What is confounding is the lack of interest from us, the repeatedly injured party, who don't seem to have the time or inclination to learn about the one subject that would protect us in many ways from being injured and taken advantage of. Could it be that we are so inured to the situation that we no longer even realise that things could be different?

Could we be so blinded with the short-term gains and instant gratification that we are unable to look ahead and recognise the toxic financial fallout we will be subject to, time and time again, even when we see it play out daily in the lives of those around us? Or so overwhelmed by the short-term cost, effort and time commitment of changing things that we knowingly trade this for blissful ignorance and inaction?

Whatever reason we choose to rationalise this for our-selves, we need to think deep and hard about using the same flawed reasoning when it comes to our teenagers. We need to remember that the system isn't broken, it was built this way. It was built to benefit those on one side of the wealth gap, while deliberately disadvantaging those on the other end of this yawning, ever widening crevice.

We need to shake ourselves out of this reverie and take some definitive steps to change things. No one else has as much to lose, except our teenagers.

Fifty shades

So far in this book, I have waxed lyrical about the benefits of giving our teenagers a proper financial education. It's time for some shades of grey. While financial education is critically important and a requirement of financial empowerment, it's also important to realise that it isn't a magic bullet against poverty and economic hardship.

There are many socio-economic and political issues, particularly affecting the economically marginalised individuals and groups – which are equally, if not more important – that need to be addressed urgently.

Unfortunately, many financial education programmes tend to frame financial wellbeing from an individualistic viewpoint, putting the onus completely on the individual while conveniently, and perhaps simplistically, ignoring the complex and compelling effect of the socio-economic and political forces at play.

In the bloody aftermath of the 2008 financial crisis, it was widely suggested that it was the financial literacy standards of the general public that were to blame, while handily ignoring the illegal behaviour of many financial institutions and the lack of appropriate government oversight.

People should have known better, they said, even as the executives of the financial institutions who were responsible for the crisis were paid millions in bonuses, while millions of ordinary people lost their homes, many more lost their jobs and the individual taxpayers were left holding the bag.

When the COVID-19 pandemic caused a financial meltdown, there again came the familiar cry, blaming this on the lack of financial literacy of the general populace and their irresponsible financial behaviour. It is naive to assume that if people are financially educated they will automatically work their way to wealth and financial security, irrespective of the major social, political and economic factors they are subject to. It's Machiavellian to make people believe that.

The mainstream financial literacy narrative is that poor decision-making, due to a lack of proper financial education, is the root cause of poverty. It blithely ignores the fact that financial wellbeing is a tall order when your pay cheque barely covers your basic needs. *Scarcity*, the provocative book by Sendhil Mullainathan and Eldar Shafir, details cutting-edge research that suggests the opposite of the mainstream narrative. Scarcity, they say, in this context of money, 'diminishes mental bandwidth – making us less insightful, less forward thinking, less controlled. Being poor reduces a person's cognitive capacity more than going one full night without sleep.' They argue that it isn't that the poor as individuals do not have as much bandwidth, rather it is the experience of poverty that reduces anyone's bandwidth. This reduced bandwidth is the reason their financial decisions aren't on point, thus exacerbating their existing financial woes. I love the way this effectively torpedoes the mainstream narrative.

We can't use the call for more financial literacy programmes and higher financial literacy standards to be used as a smokescreen to obfuscate the real issues. The racial and gender income gap is real. The social class gap is real. The wealth gap is real.

We can't claim that financial literacy will compensate for what needs to be recognised as social justice problems. Our response has to be more considered, more nuanced and more inclusive, not just a knee-jerk call for more educated consumers.

Financial literacy isn't a salvo for stagnant salaries and income inequalities and we should be wary of any personal finance gurus peddling this version of a quick fix. These so-called gurus would have us believe that our obsession with lattes, avocado toast and the like is what's pushing us over the financial cliff, but this bears no relation to economic reality. As Elizabeth Warren and her daughter Amelia Warren Tyagi reveal in their book *The Two-Income Trap*, it was the fixed costs – housing, healthcare and education – the things that are difficult to cut back on, that are the issue.

Think of that in conjunction with salaries that haven't kept up with inflation and the social safety net that is slowing disappearing and you begin to get a feel of the scale of the problem. Recognising this allows us to have a wider perspective on the subject and to, in turn, share this wider perspective with our teenagers. Not only so that they are more discerning about the financial education tips and advice they hear but also so they realise the complexity of the issues involved.

I also hope this helps build empathy in them and a willingness and determination to play a part in fighting these social injustices. If you're reading this book, chances are you're fortunate enough not to have to worry too much about social class or economic disparities affecting your teenagers. That would be a mistake. We – all of us – have a stake in the future and a collective responsibility to better it. A future that has burgeoning economic inequality is not going to be a secure one, for anyone.

It's important that we carefully consider these shades of grey when educating our teenagers about money.

For tech's sake

We mentioned in an earlier chapter that there is an app for everything, but in my view not everything needs an app. I know this is a disconcerting message, especially in our uber-tech-enabled world. Education apps in particular seem to be launched with a lot of fanfare and promises of maximising impact and unlocking potential, but we should stop and consider whether it's necessary or worthwhile to tech-enable some things. Financial education for teenagers is a case in point.

This can't be taught with a set of formulae and pre-recorded videos and tested by multiple-choice questions. This approach leaves out two other equally important aspects: behaviour and mindset. Apps, PowerPoint presentations and pre-recorded videos don't build rapport, foster trusting relationships or promote accountability.

Make no mistake, these qualities are inextricably linked to positive learning outcomes and an enjoyable learning experience – especially for teenagers. While videos and presentations could work well as additional resources, the issue arises when these are the mainstay of programme delivery. It isn't fair to the teenagers for us to assume that we can pre-package this important learning.

Teens don't learn from just listening or reading. They learn by asking thoughtful questions and getting equally thoughtful answers, by actively discussing the grey areas in the subject and by debating different points of view, which opens their minds up to ideas they'd never previously considered.

There is little that competes with a live programme facilitator who sees teens and knows them, gauges engagement levels and uses an arsenal of tactics to improve this, if needed. The facilitator can then sense confusion, despair and disinterest as accurately as she can sense interest, excitement and curiosity. She can promote a feeling of trust and accountability while expertly weaving the individual student narratives into a complex web of experience and group learning. This gives the students a sense of agency over their own learning, knowing they can direct the discussion towards a particular topic, ask questions about a specific situation and get advice on issues they might be grappling with at the moment.

Once teens realise how crucially important whatever they are learning is to their future success, they can draw on powerful intrinsic motivation, which beats the extrinsic kind hands-down any day of the week.

Let's also consider that our teens are already drowning in dopamine from being hyperconnected on their phones. According to Dr Anna Lembke in her New York Times bestselling book, *Dopamine Nation: Finding Balance in the Age of Indulgence*, this dopamine overdose is one of the leading causes of teen anxiety and depression. It's difficult enough to get them off their phones – the last thing we need is for our teenagers to get constant messages, push notifications and reminders to interact with another online platform, even if it does purportedly teach them about money.

Let's not insult their intelligence by buying into the mainstream belief that teens today have short attention spans and therefore the best way to teach them is to hit them with twenty- to thirty-second videos that attempt to oversimplify and teach them hairy financial concepts while rapping to the latest hits. Teens have a keen appreciation for honesty and authenticity. They need us to 'be real' and talk honestly about the complexities inherent in the subject. They have an intelligence and consciousness that's unrivalled and they need us to figure out how to leverage that.

Teens have immense focusing power and an innate curiosity that facilitates new learning and just need us to take the time and effort to nurture it intentionally. However technophilic Gen Z is, using tech for tech's sake isn't the answer.

STUDENT VOICE – ARIANNA

Arianna was fifteen and already quite a spender. She used her dad's credit card pretty much without a second thought. Her parents worried continuously about giving her money because she burned through it so quickly. After doing the KFI programme, Arianna said that the way she thought about money had been transformed. She noticed major changes in herself because she is now so much in control of what she spends her money on. She has now stopped impulse buying and has saved herself so much as a result.

'I make it a point to use cash. That way I'm doubly mindful of how much I'm spending,' she said, 'and I have become so responsible about my spending. My parents are quite shocked at the change they see in me.'

She even taught what she had learned to someone else – her parents. Now she feels free to weigh in on family financial decisions because of all she has learned. She feels different about her future too: 'More confident, bolder with my decisions.'

Arianna wants a career in public health as she's noticed how the socially disadvantaged seem to bear the brunt of any healthcare issue and wants to work to help change that. She feels that's a great intersection of her interest in business, economics and healthcare.

Summary

It is vital that teenagers are encouraged to adopt rebel thinking – to think independently so that they are not boxed in by current structures and rules. This way of operating will help them critically evaluate information or advertisements they come across about money-making or investment schemes that are specifically targeted at older teens.

In this chapter we discovered why technology is not the answer to a lack of financial education because teens learn through questioning, discussion and debate so that they can open their minds to new ideas.

In the next chapter we will look at whether change in financial education for teenagers is about to happen and, if and when it does, what you as a parent need to look out for when choosing a financial education programme for your teen.

SIX

With Great Power Comes Great Responsibility

In this chapter we will look at how likely it is that change in the financial education space is imminent. We also discuss the red flags to look out for in financial education programmes and how we parents should use our voices to bring about change.

A series of unfortunate events

Knowing what we now do about how important it is that our teens get a good financial education, how likely do I think it is that things are going to change in the near future?

It pains me to say this, but change is unfortunately not likely for a number of reasons. The school workload for teens is getting heavier; they are more stressed about exams and entrance tests than ever before. This pressure gives them a sort of tunnel vision where they narrowly focus on just that, not on anything that falls outside of that tunnel.

Financial education falls outside of that tunnel. There is no immediate need and/or benefit that they are aware of. Parents of teenagers are also stressed about their teens acing exams and doing well academically. They reinforce the tunnel vision and the need to focus on the existing school curriculum at the expense of all else.

Again, financial education falls by the wayside. Even when parents do recognise the benefits of a financial education, their teens resist the additional demands that would make on their time and so fight hard to get out of being enrolled in a programme. Most parents willingly stay out of confrontational situations that they feel aren't worth the fight. When push comes to shove, many parents feel that financial education isn't worth the fight.

Schools aren't going to voluntarily curate and implement the financial education curriculum. They have constraints with time, resources and budgets that aren't going to be easily solved. If, on the off chance, this is taught in school, the way it is usually taught and the relevance and relatability of the content make all the difference. Most programmes fall way short on these important criteria, hence the surveys that show how little impact these programmes have. There goes another chance of financial education impacting lives in the way it's meant to.

Around the world, financial institutions and fintech companies are stepping in to fill this yawning gap. It's tough to overlook the big red conflict-of-interest flag here: our teens are being financially educated by the companies they should be taught scepticism towards. That's before we get to the actual effectiveness of these efforts.

It's tough to imagine a couple of mind-numbing student guides and insipid PowerPoint slides with an overly patronising voiceover stuck on the website under the 'Financial Education' tab having a modicum of effect on changing the financial behaviour and impacting the financial mindset of teenagers. Do they imagine that these teens will log onto their website and take time out of their extremely busy and infinitely more interesting lives to listen to a recording of someone lecturing them on compound interest? Not bloody likely. There is no accountability, no interaction and no rapport. Hardly the magic formula for effective and enduring change and learning in teenagers.

Now the influencers on social media purporting to financially educate the younger generation with their snazzy Instagram reels and thirty-second TikTok videos are making an impact, but not necessarily a good one. Many of their posts are sponsored by the financial companies whose products they endorse and, most of the time, they hardly understand – there is that familiar red flag again. Even if it's not sponsored by a financial institution, they faithfully spout the disclaimer that what they say does not constitute financial advice.

The rest of the world sits by passively, rationalising that youngsters nowadays have short attention spans and this is maybe the best way to get through to them, never stopping to consider that many of the 'finfluencers' are neither trained nor subject to any regulation and hence are not the best people our teenagers should be learning from.

Again, due to a series of unfortunate events, financial education in its truest sense is the casualty and our woefully unprepared teens are collateral damage. Therefore, let the buyer beware of what you might be signing your teenagers up for.

Caveat emptor

Caveat emptor is Latin for 'let the buyer beware' – a phrase that holds particular significance when enrolling your teens in a financial education programme. It is up to you as a parent to make an informed choice about which financial education programme your teen will be impacted by. Keep in mind that this isn't a subject you want your teen to have just a passing knowledge of. This isn't about choosing one that's just satisfactory. Your teen's knowledge and expertise on the subject will influence so many critical aspects of their lives. 'Satisfactory' won't cut it here; it needs to be exceptional.

You don't want someone playing fast and loose with the foundations and principles of smart money management and investing. The programme you choose needs:

- To have been tested on thousands of students and be better for it

- To go far beyond just building awareness to focusing on the implementation of the learning

- To challenge your teen to think differently and then act in accordance with their beliefs

- To be trusted that there will be no hidden commercial agendas your teen will be subject to.

There's been a lot of talk about the net effectiveness of financial education programmes, which according to some studies is marginal, if non-existent. Frankly, that's not surprising. If you take a look at the way many financial education programmes are run, in terms of the content they cover and their delivery process, it's a far from surprising conclusion.

From simplistic perspectives and volunteer staff who aren't trained to teach teens to shameless product pushing and content that is unabashedly commercially coloured, there is a lot to beware of. Caveat emptor!

Then there is the actual content, which is tedious, uninteresting and mainly taught as a maths-based skill. Personal finance isn't a maths-based skill; it has much to do with mindset, attitude and behaviour. Yet behavioural finance and an understanding of the interplay of various socio-economic factors isn't covered. Caveat emptor!

Parents should be especially aware of financial education programmes taught by financial institutions. According to the FoolProof Foundation website, today's financial literacy education 'doesn't work because virtually all major financial literacy resources are developed or shaped by businesses that benefit when consumers make money mistakes.' It's like the fox being asked to guard the chicken coop. Caveat emptor!

There's nothing wrong with financial institutions sponsoring financial education programmes in schools and colleges; that might be a solution to the budgetary issue most schools claim to have when faced with teaching this subject on their own. The problem arises when these financial institutions flog their own 'bespoke curriculum', highlighting their products and services targeted at teens.

One solution would be to have financial education programmes curated and delivered by a vetted independent third party of trained and trusted experts. This would ensure that the students get the benefit of the programmes without being subject to implicit or explicit marketing messages. It would also ensure a quality standard and unbiased content. Financial education, and more importantly financial empowerment, isn't just a score on a 'three-question quiz'. While that might be a basic measure, it does not even begin to cover what we need our teens to know, understand and use about money.

Especially in today's time, our definition of what constitutes a financial education needs to change dramatically – it needs to provide our teens with deep insights, an evolved understanding and a higher consciousness about money.

This means that an exceptional financial education programme needs to go beyond the basic elements that most programmes run through. It needs to encompass the new and evolving components of technology, social media influences, neuroeconomics and the aforementioned behavioural finance and interplay of various socio-economic factors.

Rather than giving teens a quick recipe for financial success, it needs to provide them with a solid foundation in finance and the basic principles to allow them to think for themselves and make sense of the constantly and rapidly changing financial landscape. It needs to give teens a sense of control and agency over their own future.

Such a well-rounded and holistic programme, expertly delivered, is exactly what we require for our teens. Anything else is playing into the narrative of a financial programme with marginal utility.

All in all, caveat emptor is a handy phrase to keep in mind when evaluating your teens' first brush with this life-changing subject.

As a result of the financial fallout of the COVID-19 pandemic, governments, financial institutions, schools and universities everywhere are taking concrete steps to boost financial literacy scores worldwide. Aside from mandating institutional changes in the academic curriculums, companies will be held accountable for their marketing tactics, and any predatory marketing targeting teens will be severely penalised.

Both educational and financial institutions worldwide have welcomed these changes with open arms and, more importantly, with detailed implementation plans, complete with hard deadlines and effectiveness checks. Schools, colleges and universities around the world have made sweeping changes to how kids and teens are taught about money. They've realised how critical this skill is to develop early and they are committed to doing just that. Finally, this important subject is getting the spotlight it deserves.

Not content to wait for corporate sponsorships, educational institutions are allocating funds specifically to further students' understanding of all things money. The effect of these systemic changes is a financially empowered generation that has relegated financial naivety to the annals of history.

No, wait. That didn't happen. Don't hold your breath. It won't. Not without your voice.

Let's get loud

As parents, we have a real stake in this enduring and intractable issue and we must realise that we have a powerful voice too, should we choose to use it.

Most educational institutions aren't going to make changes of their own volition, at least not in the immediate future. They will cite 'budgetary constraints' at every opportunity, irrespective of the fact that these schools charge exorbitant fees. This means another generation will be forced to learn too little, too late, about a subject that's critically important to their future.

As it is, according to GW Media Relations in their blog post 'Gen Z has the lowest financial literacy, study reveals', Gen Z have lower financial literacy scores than Gen X or Y or Boomers.

Companies aren't going to stop using predatory marketing tactics on our teens. They are just too lucrative a market, not to mention financially clueless too, by some happy coincidence. That's marketing gold. From stock and forex trading sites to online gambling and gaming, these companies blitz through disclaimers of their addictive nature in their advertisements, while highlighting the opportunity to 'get lucky/get rich' or some gimmicky version thereof.

Governments admittedly have bigger problems on their hands, so educating kids and teens about money seems relatively unimportant. If only they realised the harmful repercussions to society as a result of bad money decisions, maybe they'd rethink their priorities. From rising rates of financial scams and ballooning consumer debt to non-existent savings and a distinct lack of wealth-building activity – this seemingly unimportant problem has tentacles squeezing the core of a stable society.

Our only real hope for immediate and lasting change lies with parents everywhere. It's up to us to ensure our teens get a proper financial education, not the tick-the-box variety but one that fosters lasting change.

On school boards, at PTA meetings, at every interaction with educational authorities, we need to bring this simmering issue to the front and tackle it head on. No more accepting lame rationalisations from schools. No more waiting for someone else to speak up.

We have a voice, one that we need to use to protect and safeguard our teens from a future riddled with financial strife. Let's get loud.

A matter of time

Teens spend around ten hours a day getting to and attending class and another couple of hours snowed under with homework – that's a minimum of twelve hours in school-related time per day. Take eight hours off for sleep, which should be a minimum requirement, and most teens are left with a measly four hours a day to shower, eat, relax…and then fit in a host of other extracurricular activities. School is monopolising our teenagers' time, so maybe we should all look a little deeper into the best use of that time.

With schools taking up the lion's share of available time in their lives, it's only logical and fair that they deal with the critical aspect of preparing teenagers for adult life – that is, after all, the whole point of school – and financial empowerment ranks highly in this preparedness.

Most parents everywhere would agree that financial empowerment is a critical life skill and would be relieved, pleased and extremely grateful if schools took it upon themselves to empower teenagers with the said skill.

Yet, aside from the funds and resources, many schools say they don't have time to financially educate their students. Therein lies the real tragedy. How short-sighted and oblivious to the inherent danger this poses does one have to be to take this stance?

I don't even want to get into the myriad useless and redundant classes most students have to attend during their educational journey. It seems that the real tragedy of an outdated curriculum are the critical things that students don't have the time to learn.

Keep in mind that the time spent in school is not just any time, it's at a crucial juncture of growth when teen brain development is at its maximum – anything they learn now, they learn quicker and more effectively than at any other time in their lives. Schools also have the added benefit of having the teenager's social circle – learning which has this social element is more memorable and thus more effective.

Schools have everything lined up perfectly for them: teens spend so much time there, their brains are primed to learn at this time in their lives, and having their social circle around helps to activate learning pathways in their brain.

While I know that it's common to refer to the twenties as the defining decade in a person's life, it's the decade prior to the twenties that deserves that distinction. Because it's during that prior decade that they learn what they need to, that they fuel up for the ride. Since most of that decade is spent in education, it falls upon schools to get our teens ready for the world. One can't be world ready if one has no concept of how money works.

We think of youngsters as having loads of time, and they believe it themselves too. They procrastinate about learning how to deal with money smartly and how to invest for the long term, but we've all seen how time seems to pass in a blink of an eye.

It's said that with great power comes great responsibility...schools don't only have great power, they are also privy to a great amount of our teens' time, and that surely comes with an even greater responsibility.

STUDENT VOICE – MARIAM

Although Mariam, a nineteen-year-old university student, was careful with money, she realised that there was so much more she needed to learn about. It all seemed too complex. Personal finance wasn't covered in her university. They only learned corporate finance and about annuities and perpetuity, all of which seemed so far removed from what she needed to know about money on a daily basis.

After the KFI programme, Mariam said she was clearer about money. In particular, she said that what she learned about emergency funds hit home, especially because the pandemic had caused a lot of financial upheaval in her family. She understood the value of planning ahead and for the long term.

She loved putting what she'd learned into practice. In fact, she even budgeted for her birthday party for the first time. 'It gave me such a sense of pride and accomplishment when I managed that successfully. I know it's a small example, but it built up my confidence to take on bigger challenges.'

'I'm so much wiser and more aware when it comes to marketing tactics used by companies and it pains me to see my friends being so gullible and falling for these tactics.'

Mariam plans on doing her master's degree but is adamant that she's going to finance it herself. 'I think my parents have done more than enough, it's time for me to step up and now I have a much clearer picture of how I can do that.'

Summary

In this chapter we have looked at the possibility that the provision of financial education in schools will change in the future. The answer is that financial companies and fintech are stepping in to plug this gap instead.

We've also investigated the key elements that make up a good financial programme for teens. Of course, we know that change won't happen easily and it is up to us as parents to get our voices heard so that we can change the future for our teenagers.

In the next chapter we will look at our five-step blueprint that will change the way teenagers are financially literate.

SEVEN

The Crucial Five-step Blueprint

Financial education for teenagers is an extremely emotive topic. While everyone readily agrees it is a critical life skill that teens must be taught, there hasn't been much (or any) thought put into the best way to teach it. That's the only way one can explain the narrow focus, abysmally dry content and ineffective delivery of most financial education programmes targeted at teens. It's like we are willing them to fall asleep or curse their luck for being stuck in yet another class that they find absolutely no joy in. Make no mistake, for any learning to be effective there needs to be joy.

I have looked long and hard into the problems surrounding this issue and have now crystallised my methodology into a five-step blueprint that revolutionises the way financial education is taught to teens. The five steps are:

1. Recognising the gap
2. Reasoning with them
3. Relating to them
4. Raising the bar
5. Reflecting with them

Each of these steps is crucial; not just for the effectiveness and impact of the programme but also, equally importantly, to ensure a thoroughly enjoyable learning process for the students.

Step 1: Recognising the gap

For teens, financial education is an unconscious incompetence, as we discussed in Chapter 2. Teens don't know that they don't know about money. They are clueless about their inability to handle money smartly and are blissfully unaware of how crucially important this skill is for their future success and wellbeing. What makes this more dangerous is the Dunning-Kruger effect – a cognitive bias in which people with a low ability at a task overestimate their ability at that task.

Not only do teens not know that they don't know about money, they also typically tend to overestimate their ability to make smart money decisions. They assume they know all about money just because they have a debit or credit card or can track their expenses on an app, or because they have learned to trade stocks online. In fact, having a debit or credit card and dabbling in stocks without some foundational financial education is dangerous and ill-advised.

There is a double curse of the Dunning-Kruger effect: since teens are unaware of this gap in their knowledge, they don't take any steps to remedy it. They might, in fact, actively resist the opportunity to learn how to handle money smartly because they assume they already do.

We need to ensure that as educators or parents we recognise this gap in their knowledge. Because of our blind spots, which I have mentioned previously, we tend to assume that they know more about money than they do.

We also need to beware of a common cognitive bias here – the confirmation bias – where we tend to only recall information in a way that confirms our prior beliefs. Consequently, we only see instances that prove to us that our teens are good with money, while ignoring evidence to the contrary.

In addition, we need to recognise the bias in our teens' thinking. This goes a long way in understanding and empathising with their initial lack of interest or initiative in learning about the topic of money. It's our job to take them from 'unconscious incompetence' to 'unconscious competence', where they become so skilled at managing money it becomes second nature to them. Whatever steps and actions we take in teaching them about money can and will dramatically affect their financial success.

Therefore, while they may not initially be favourably inclined to learn about money, it's up to us to help them overcome this starting problem. We need to recognise our power in guiding them onto the right path.

Step 2: Reasoning with them

The sight is the same in most classes in school and college: the disengaged body language and looks of utter boredom and disinterest on the faces of teens. They sit through the drudgery, waiting for the sound of the bell, when they get a few minutes of freedom before they get to do this all over again, with equal enthusiasm. One of the reasons for this in the context of their financial education is that they don't know why they are being taught all of this in the first place, aside from the fact that it could be on the exam.

This adversely affects their motivation, which takes a nosedive and never recovers, but all we need to do is tell them why. As author Simon Sinek says in his book *Start With Why*, we need to take the time to explain why this skill is so critical for their future success.

Most teens are quite worried about their future. They've seen the pandemic-induced recession – close up and in technicolour – ravage the livelihoods of millions of people worldwide, and this has understandably heightened their anxiety. They realise that they are going to graduate into a tough economy and they feel quite ill-equipped to face this. When teens know why they have to learn something and how they will benefit, they are much more motivated to learn. Self-interest kicks in, and they try harder and keep at it for longer. After all, intrinsic motivation always trumps the extrinsic kind.

Studies by neuroscientist Dr Silvia Bunge from the University of California, Berkeley, show that motivation is experienced in the brain as a release of dopamine, enhancing the signalling of neurons. The motivated brain operates better and signals faster. When teenagers are motivated, they learn better.

We take this one step further when we tell teens in class that they don't have to do any of the tasks we set for them if they don't see the utility in what we ask them to do. We tell them that it's our responsibility to convince them of the 'why' of everything, and we take that responsibility quite seriously. The fact that almost every teen completes the tasks we set them is testament to the fact that this works.

Teenagers aren't used to being told why, but they catch on quickly once they see how much more enjoyable learning is when the 'why' behind it is clear. It also gets teens into a habit of questioning and looking for the 'why' in everything they learn. This can only be a good thing. When the why is clear, the how is easy.

Step 3: Relating to them

By the time most kids hit their teen years, they feel disconnected from most of their teachers and find it hard to relate to them. This goes both ways. Teens are the most challenging age group to teach because they think they already know everything (the truth notwithstanding) and because of a second issue that's tougher to grapple with. In their book *NurtureShock*, Po Bronson and Ashley Merryman write about the work of neuroscientist Dr Adriana Galván who says 'there is good reason to believe that teens are neurobiologically prone to boredom. Inside our brains is a reward centre, which lights up with dopamine whenever we find something interesting or exciting or pleasurable.' In a study comparing the brains of teens to the brains of adults and young kids, Galván found that teen brains can't get pleasure out of doing things that are only mildly or moderately rewarding.

This poses a challenge for teachers as they have to be intriguing, innovative and fun – all of the time. The content being taught also needs to be immensely interesting to them. Being even slightly off your game means that the teens slip into catatonic boredom, and that's not easy to get them back from.

It's more than that, though. We need to take the time to build a relationship with them. Kids, irrespective of their age, don't have a favourite subject, they have a favourite teacher. If they like the teacher they like the subject, and unfortunately the reverse is true as well. Relatedness is a fundamental need for teens.

Teens get a high from connecting with people and developing a sense of belonging. It provides them with a sense of security and wellbeing; whereas a lack of connectedness correlates to stress, depression and loneliness. Getting to know the teens in class – what they're looking forward to, what they're anxious about and what makes them happy – is a sure-fire way to build this elusive feeling.

The content also needs to be relevant to their lives now, solving problems they can foresee having and benefits they can clearly picture in the not-so-distant future. Talk about mortgages, pensions and retirement and you've lost them at hello. Guess what most personal finance classes in school teach? Yes, exactly that.

Once they see the relevance of the content, they can't help but be interested, engaged and committed to the learning process. Build in some fun and humour and you've got the proverbial icing on the cake.

Step 4: Raising the bar

Most financial education programmes tend to focus exclusively on building financial knowledge. They focus on tactical issues like saving and spending, while neglecting the more strategic ones. Their aim is to raise awareness. Awareness alone isn't enough, or effective. Just because someone knows the right thing to do, doesn't mean they will do it. Smokers know the harmful effects of cigarettes but still continue to smoke. If we want to effect true change, we need to raise the bar and focus on mindset and behaviour, which are arguably as important as knowledge.

Influencing mindset and behaviour takes more time and effort, but financial education is not something you want your teens to rush through. You wouldn't want the effect of the programme to be fleeting. It defeats the purpose of teaching them this 'life skill' that ensures lasting change.

The confluence of these three aspects – knowledge, behaviour and mindset – underpins a truly effective programme. We help the teens discover and mould a mindset around money that serves them: one that is positive and free from limiting beliefs. As Morgan Housel states in his book *The Psychology of Money*, 'financial success is not a hard science. It's a soft skill where how you behave is more important than what you know.'

We show the teens how to change their behaviour based on the financial concepts we teach. We get them to notice and celebrate even small changes, because those small changes will compound over time. They don't just learn about compounding and how to calculate it, they get to understand how compounding works in every aspect of their life.

This is a revelation for most teens, for whom compound interest is just an abstract concept in their maths textbooks. They learn that good investing isn't necessarily about earning the highest returns, because as Housel says, 'the highest returns tend to be one-off hits that can't be repeated. It's about earning pretty good returns that you can stick with and which can be repeated for the longest period of time.' That, Housel says, 'is when compounding runs wild'.

During this step, teens delve into other people's experiences, and help them crystallise valuable lessons about mindset and behaviour from those stories. Working on their mindset, giving them the knowledge and then incorporating specific behavioural changes is where the magic is. Each aspect compounds the effect of the other two, making the combination of all three exponentially more powerful and long lasting.

Another important aspect of raising the bar is to include two oft-ignored facets of financial education: gratitude and generosity. Taking time to slow down and appreciate what we have – that's priceless.

Artfully incorporating that into a conversation with teens takes a bit of creativity, but the effects of any gratitude-building activity are fascinating, especially when teens see for themselves how powerful it can be.

Generosity too plays a crucial part in financial education. We need to instil a higher consciousness in teens. This is relatively easy to do because most teens today have a finely honed sense of fairness that is easy to extrapolate into generosity. Aside from being hugely valuable in their own right, these two facets of gratitude and generosity also have an important impact on financial wellbeing and shouldn't be ignored.

Step 5: Reflecting with them

Student reflection is integral to any learning experience and unfortunately is often left out of the equation. When the emphasis is placed on content coverage, teens passively absorb facts and miss out on a crucial element of deep learning. When they don't have time to reflect, this impacts their ability to use what they have learned effectively and has the knock-on effect of thwarting their motivation and interest levels.

The solution to this is to encourage students to reflect on their learning and think about whatever they have learned, what skills they have developed as a result of that learning, how they can use these skills in their everyday life, and what would have happened if they hadn't learned what they did. This helps them make the important connections between what they've learned academically and how they will get to use what they've learned, reinforcing 'why' they learn the various topics.

This, in particular, seems to be a real eye-opener for the teens, when they realise the credit card debt they would have inadvertently gotten into, the bad debt they would have unwisely taken on with a car loan for a spanking-new car, or the speculative activities they would have engaged in, thinking they were 'investing'. This is crucial for them to be able to develop insights and think critically about the subject.

They become aware of what skills need to be refined further and how they can make that happen. That leads to self-directed learning, which is powerful. They might, for example, decide that they need to further their knowledge about the intricacies of budgeting, or maybe they want to learn more about investing intelligently.

Reflection is also a key ingredient to move knowledge from short- to long-term memory. As John Dewey says in 'Reflection: How do I do it?', 'We don't learn from experience. We learn from reflecting on experience.' It's how effective learning happens. That's why reflection plays such an important part in our teaching processes.

Effectively teaching teens about money is too critical an issue to leave to guesswork, lazy assumptions or a throw of the dice. We get just one formal shot at it before the teens stumble headlong into adulthood where this skill can be a complete game changer. It's our responsibility to make sure we nail it perfectly.

By using the blueprint detailed in this chapter – of recognising the gap, reasoning with them, relating to them, raising the bar and reflecting with them – we do just that.

STUDENT VOICE – RIZWAN

Rizwan is a twenty-year-old university student currently working as a summer intern. He is a professional athlete and used to make a bit of sponsorship money but never thought about how he was spending it. He wasted most of his money buying stuff he hardly used.

He realised he was clueless and unprepared to handle money, just as many of his friends and colleagues were, with many of them holding unpaid balances on their credit cards. He read a couple of the standard personal finance books and even watched a number of videos relating to personal finance. Since attending the KFI programme, he now advises his friends on smart spending.

He'd also just been given his driver's licence and realised that, prior to attending the programme, he would have taken out a car loan and bought a brand-new expensive car without thinking about whether that was the best use of his money and whether he needed to take on so much debt unnecessarily.

Now, he even helps his parents budget and is involved in the financial decisions his family take, whether big or small. 'They've noticed how I have changed, especially with regard to reining in my impulse purchases, and seem to value my input,' he says.

Summary

In this chapter we have covered the five-step blueprint of the KFI programme:

1. Recognising the gap

2. Reasoning with them

3. Relating to them

4. Raising the bar

5. Reflecting with them.

Using this model will ensure that the teens' first brush with financial education is impactful, engaging and effective.

In the next chapter we will look at models we incorporate into our teaching which help teenagers to think differently, engage more and learn effectively.

EIGHT

Effective Teen Teaching Methods

In this chapter I discuss how useful it is to teach teens to think differently and critically. I take you through our ideology and ethos, and introduce several models that will enrich and enhance the teen learning experience. I also investigate whether teens benefit from the indiscriminate use of technology in teaching. Let's start with the first model I use in my teaching: The Triple-T model.

The Triple-T model

When it comes to teaching teens about personal finance there's not much difference in 'what' is taught by various entities who take on this task. There are tons of books and resources available, detailing what should be covered – ranging from needs, wants and spending styles to budgeting and compound interest – which means there's a universal commonality to the content being taught.

We have, however, expanded on the usual content to include topics and aspects that are both intriguing and compelling, such as behavioural finance and investing, and we teach them in a way that is both fascinating and enjoyable for teenagers.

As I mentioned before, this isn't a skill we want our teens to learn just to tick the proverbial box; given how crucial and life-changing this skill is, we need them to willingly absorb the learning, effectively retain it and then efficiently implement it. To do this, we have developed the Triple-T model, which involves three stages: Train, Teach and Try it out.

Let's dive into each stage individually:

- **Train:** Whatever we teach teens serves to train their RAS (Reticular Activation System) to be more aware about situations involving money. This builds their awareness around the topic so that they pay more attention to conversations around money and are sensitised to circumstances that involve it. As a result, they are more mindful about what they spend it on and other money decisions they make. This step alone is extremely powerful, as it gets them to think differently about money.

- **Teach:** We encourage teens to commit to teaching everything they learned to at least one other person. In this step, they teach, they learn twice and they learn better because going over the content while teaching it is a great way for them to efficiently revise and thus reinforce the content. The feedback and reaction they get from the person they teach plays a big role in cementing the effectiveness of this strategy.

- **Try it out:** This makes the learning tangible. When I end each session with how the teens can now practically use this information in their everyday lives, it brings their learning to life. This dramatically increases their motivation because they see how it benefits them, which makes them eager to put what they've learned into practice. It's important to do this for each concept of the programme as it emphasises its usefulness, again serving to buttress their engagement and motivation.

Each of the Ts are powerful and effective in their own right, but together they serve to leverage the entire learning process by actively engaging teens with the content, not just passively absorbing it.

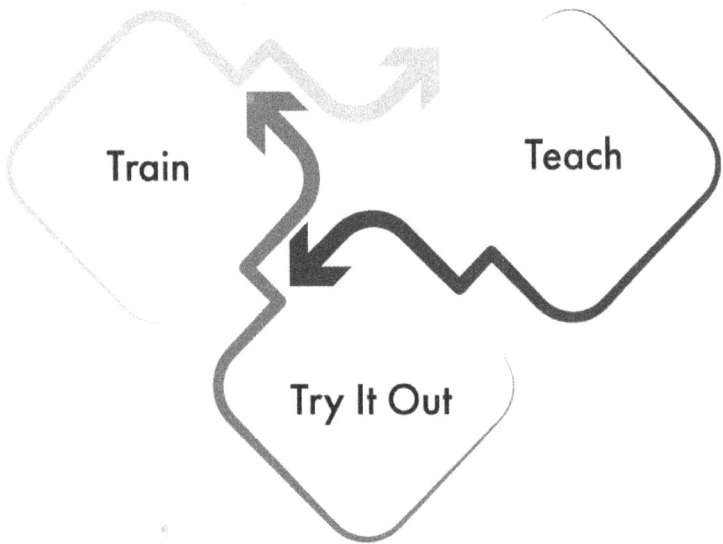

R.A.P.I.D. transformation

Our next model is called the R.A.P.I.D. transformation model, which I have formulated over the years of educating students about money. The steps of the model are:

- Revise

- Advise

- Personalise

- Internalise

- Devise

This works in tandem with the Triple-T model explained in the previous section and leads to quick and lasting change.

Taking each step in turn:

- **Revise:** Revision of content previously covered is key, especially as this isn't taught as a test-oriented subject. Going over the main concepts covered in the last session does a lot to scaffold the upcoming lesson while reinforcing past content. This is particularly important with financial education because each topic builds upon the previous one and is critical for an in-depth understanding of the subject as a whole. As this is likely to be the first and only time these teens will undergo formal training on the subject, it's doubly important that the concepts are explained and understood well. Repetition gets them to look at the content with fresh eyes, in light of what they've covered since, and gain new insights.

- **Advise:** Here students review real case studies and I ask them what they would advise the person in the case study to do. Asking them how they would advise someone to solve a problem gets them thinking critically. It helps them to draw from their recent learnings and find ways to implement these concepts. Giving advice also unconsciously makes them behave congruently to this advice in their own lives. When teens repeatedly think in this mode, it helps them to recognise patterns quicker so they respond better when faced with these situations in real life.

- **Personalise:** It is important to personalise content where possible. For example, if a student is studying to be a chef and dreams of opening their own restaurant, or is soon going off to university and living on their own, we personalise the examples to suit their particular situation. This gets their attention as they are now seeing the content from a personal point of view, which makes it more relevant and interesting to them. It also gets them to engage with the material in a way that's more meaningful and ultimately more memorable, which has the added benefit of building richer relationships as students feel seen as individuals, not just a class as a whole. This makes for more involved and committed students.

- **Internalise:** This is where students become so well-versed in the topics that they have moved from 'unconscious incompetence' (where they didn't know that they didn't know) to a place of 'unconscious competence'. They have become so good at this skill that it is now second nature to them. It's like riding a bike – they don't have to think about their actions and movements when they are riding. With regard to money, they no longer have to consciously think hard about their decisions. They automatically make the right ones because they have internalised the learnings so well and are implementing these learnings on a regular basis. This doesn't mean they are less mindful; it means it takes less effort for them to make the right decisions. This is because they have internalised the concepts and their brains are now effectively hardwired to work in that way.

- **Devise:** Here we constantly devise ways to increase the social interactions in class. While passive learning might feel easier, active learning is a whole lot more effective and long lasting. Teens learn best by discussing, debating and asking questions. Working together in small groups makes their ideas and brain circuits come alive. They also seem to enjoy it more, which builds richer relationships with the students and also among the students. As Dr David Rock states in his book *Your Brain at Work,* 'There are additional benefits to harnessing the power of social interactions. There is a memory network that gets activated when information is social that turns out to be more robust than a memory without a social element.' Devising ways to get the teens to open up and interact with each other takes the engagement and enjoyment level up several notches and has the added impact of making the learning more memorable. Win-win all around.

My magic sauce

To make sure our teens are primed for learning and have a valuable and enjoyable learning experience, three further teaching practices set the stage perfectly.

1. Students are actively encouraged to ask questions

This gets students to focus on what they don't know. It allows them to think of the content in a different way, looking for gaps in their own understanding, which they can ask about. Getting teens to ask questions is harder than it appears for a number of reasons:

- They're not used to it. Education systems train them to answer questions, not ask them. Usually in schools, in the interest of expediency, questions branching off from the topic are either brushed off or frowned upon. Flipping the script and getting them to think about what questions they can ask or what else they'd like to know about the topic takes a bit of getting used to. Once they do, however, they begin to see for themselves how it accelerates their learning and gives them a deeper take on the issue being discussed.

- Many teens have a carefully cultivated, cool, detached demeanour that eschews showing how interested they are in anything. It's just not cool to show you care. Asking questions shows you care enough to think about it and want to know more.

This is tricky but is easily solved once they realise how much they stand to benefit from being engaged and how much more enjoyable it is, compared to passively listening to the content. They begin to realise how every question they ask benefits the whole class because the other students were either too shy to ask themselves or had never thought about this particular aspect. This breaks down the question-asking barriers because they now see themselves as helping their fellow classmates. It's then important to take the time to acknowledge the effort they put into asking thoughtful questions.

2. I don't care whether they answer correctly

I don't, really. What I do care about is that they try and make an honest attempt at an answer when I ask questions in class. I want to encourage engagement, irrespective of whether or not they think they have the right answer. Many teens only try if they are absolutely sure they have the correct answer; they don't want to risk being ridiculed.

I want them to realise that it's OK to make a mistake – that's what effective learning is all about. This takes some getting used to because they have been conditioned by school to only answer when they are 100%

sure of the answer. Getting them to answer out loud when they are unsure means getting them to step out of their comfort zone of certainty – a difficult but worthwhile endeavour.

There is another reason we love mistakes. In the article 'Mistakes grow your brain: How to use the science of struggle to improve the learning experience', Stefanie Frank says that our brains grow when we make mistakes. Mistakes cause synapses to fire and this increases learning.

I make the teens understand that, particularly in personal finance, there is no 'one right answer' for everyone. Every person might have a different answer, based on their particular reading of the situation and how they were brought up or taught to behave. Taking out a car loan might make sense for one person while being an unwise choice for another, depending on their individual circumstances. Getting teens to take the initiative to answer in class is important because it raises the class engagement level, making it more interesting and memorable for everyone.

3. I clarify that it is my job to ensure the content I teach is easily understood

I tell the teens I teach that it's my responsibility to ensure that I explain the content as simply as possible so that it's easy for them to understand. If they don't, it just means that I haven't done such a great job of explaining the material. They need to tell me and I will try harder to remedy that.

This shows the teens they shouldn't be embarrassed or feel stupid if they're confused about what's taught in class. I explain that some kids learn differently from others and while I usually use the most common method of explanation, sometimes I need to approach the concept from a different angle.

This rule does wonders for the teens' confidence and self-esteem and they are then much more open about admitting that they didn't understand or they need additional help with something. This makes for much better learning.

All my interactions with students are based on the self-determination theory developed by psychologists Dr Richard Ryan and Dr Edward Deci, who proposed that the human psyche needs three psychological nutrients to flourish: competence, autonomy and relatedness.

- **Competence – to feel like they've done a good job:** Competence feels good and as it grows, so too does their confidence. Being more confident is a key result of the programme. The teens notice their own growth and development, which gives them a sense of achievement. There is a ton of scientific evidence to prove that the perceptual abilities and memory function of teens are far superior to those of adults. We need to trust in their abilities and give them a fair chance.

- **Autonomy – to feel like they have control over what they do:** Teens don't feel like they have much freedom over their choices and this can be disempowering. Robert Epstein, who wrote the *Scientific American* article, 'The myth of the teen brain', says that according to surveys he has conducted, teens in the US are subjected to more than ten times as many restrictions as mainstream adults and twice as many as incarcerated felons. Is it any wonder that most teens seem so unmotivated in the classroom? We deliberately eschew this sort of structure and rigidity. We don't infantilise them and it works wonders because they inevitably rise the challenge. Their motivation is then intrinsic and much more powerful than any extrinsic motivation we could provide.

- **Relatedness – to have meaningful relationships and interactions with other people:** This helps teens to thrive. They need to feel connected and cared for and to interact. Because of this I have deliberately shied away from pre-recorded and asynchronous classes. It's difficult, if not impossible, to build rapport and connection though them. Equally importantly is the interaction between students – that is where the real magic happens. We need to ensure that we are giving them enough opportunities to work together and problem-solve or ideate. It brings out the best in them.

By building these three elements into our programme, I ensure that the teens are primed to thrive.

Summary

Several models that I use in teaching teenagers have been discussed in this chapter.

First, the Triple-T model, which involves the three stages of:

- Train

- Teach

- Try it out

Secondly, working alongside this, is the R.A.P.I.D. transformation model. The steps are as follows:

- Revise

- Advise

- Personalise

- Internalise

- Devise

Finally, we covered our 'magic sauce', which ensures that our teenagers are ready to learn and have a valuable and enjoyable learning experience while doing so.

Conclusion

We need to act. Now. Let's take a last look at a couple of useful analogies that illustrate the importance of financial education for your children.

Red pill or blue pill?

Would you give your teen the red pill or the blue pill? If you're like most parents, you'd rather not do either. The less contentious the interactions we have with our teenagers, the better our mental health will be. Using an analogy from the 1999 science fiction film, *The Matrix*, imagine for a moment that you had a choice of giving them either a red pill or a blue one.

Choose the red pill and everything changes

The red pill – in this case enrolling them for a financial education course – would mean that their life gets a bit harder, requires a time commitment and would cost you money – at least in the short term. It also has the added disadvantage of your teen being initially resistant to this idea.

It will open your teen's mind to the way the world works around money. They will understand how to use this knowledge and modify their mindset and behaviour to make smarter money decisions.

Just like in the movie, this knowledge also gives them the ability to dodge the metaphorical bullet through financial self-defence, where they learn how to defend themselves against bad debt, financial scams and other fiscal pitfalls. By learning how to use the magic of compound interest, they will get a head start on building wealth. This directly results in them becoming more self-reliant and financially secure earlier in their lives. As with anything worthwhile, this involves an initial commitment of time and money, but it's plain to see that the returns are stratospheric.

Choosing the blue pill is the easy option: Nothing changes

Just as in *The Matrix*, this pill prevents your teen from discovering the truth; in this case of how most people are enslaved by money. They can go back to living in comfort and blissful ignorance. It doesn't cost you anything – at least in the short term. It has the added advantage of your teen being happier with you choosing this option, mainly because she cannot comprehend the opportunity cost now.

The downside to this choice, however, is monumental. Your teen will be condemned to commit expensive money mistakes, which aside from being financially ruinous will also carry a heavy cost in time and self-confidence. This isn't easy to recover from.

This is no science fiction. Data-backed studies show that teens who do not take a financial education course are more likely to be compulsive buyers, less likely to save and more likely to max out their credit cards.

Without financial self-defence, teens then unwittingly take on bad debt, fall victims to financial fraud and, perhaps worst of all, are late off the mark in investing wisely and building wealth. Being financially fragile then becomes unavoidable.

Next steps

I said in the introduction that this was a book I wanted to read, and that's why I wrote it. I've seen first-hand how financial empowerment can positively impact people's lives and I hope that you're convinced enough to take some definite steps to getting your teens started on their own financial empowerment journey.

Now that you've read this book, your definition of financial education will be more holistic. Your standards of what to expect in a financial education programme will be more exacting and your patience at getting this critical skill engrained in your teenagers will hopefully be wearing thin. This is a good thing. We've seen how time is of the essence in this regard and we stand to gain nothing by waiting.

The sooner they start, the sooner they will be smarter richer braver:

- **Smarter** because of their deep and nuanced understanding of money and how it works.

- **Richer** because this directly translates into added or saved wealth.

- **Braver** because armed with this skill they are able to make bolder choices.

You are effectively giving them a superpower; one that supercharges all their other skills and abilities, so that you may worry less.

Thank you for the privilege of letting me spend this time with you. I hope you will let me know of the changes you see in your teens once they've acquired this skill and the many ways they've made you proud. Because they will.

If you'd like to find out your teen's financial empowerment score, take this quick quiz at kfiglobal.scoreapp
.com. It only takes a couple of minutes, it's free and it
will also give you a few pointers on how to increase
your teen's score.

If you would like to find out about how we can help
your teenagers, you can contact us in the following
ways:

⊕ www.kfi.global

🐦 @kfiglobaltribe

🔗 www.linkedin.com/company/kfiglobaltribe

Bibliography

Blakemore, S-J and Bunge, S, 'At the nexus of neuro-science and education', *Developmental Cognitive Neuroscience*, 2/1 (2012), 1–5, https://doi.org/10.1016/j.dcn.2012.01.001

Bloomberg.com, 'Warren Buffett becomes sixth member of $100 billion club' (2021), www.bloomberg.com/news/articles/2021-03-10/warren-buffett-becomes-sixth-member-of-100-billion-club, accessed 30 March 2022

Bronson, P and Merryman, A, *NurtureShock: New thinking about children* (Twelve, 2009)

Campellone, J and Turley, RK, 'Understanding the teen brain', *University of Rochester Medical Center Health Encyclopedia*, www.urmc.rochester.edu/encyclopedia/content.aspx?ContentTypeID=1&ContentID=3051, accessed 28 March 2022

Deci, EL and Ryan, RM, *Intrinsic Motivation and Self-Determination in Human Behavior* (Plenum, 1985)

Dewey, J, 'Reflection: How do I do it?', *Teaching & Learning* (24 March 2016), https://tl.hku.hk/2016/03/reflection-how-do-i-do-it-john-dewey-we-do-not-learn-from-experience-we-learn-from-reflecting-on-experience, accessed 31 March 2022

Epstein, R, 'The myth of the teen brain', *Scientific American* (1 June 2007), www.scientificamerican.com/article/the-myth-of-the-teen-brain-2007-06, accessed 1 April 2022

Fidelity Investments, '2021 Women and Investing Study' (2021), www.fidelity.com/bin-public/060_www_fidelity_com/documents/about-fidelity/FidelityInvestmentsWomen&InvestingStudy2021.pdf, accessed 28 March 2022

FoolProof Foundation, 'More than half of millennials say they are living paycheck to paycheck' (2022), www.foolprooffoundation.org/who-we-are/why-we-exist, accessed 31 March 2022

Frank, SF, 'Mistakes grow your brain: How to use the science of struggle to improve the learning experience', *Bam Radio* (8 November 2016), www.bamradionetwork.com/mistakes-grow-your-brain-how-to-use-the-science-of-struggle-to-improve-the-learning-experience, accessed 31 March 2022

Grant, A, *Think Again* (WH Allen, 2021)

GW Media Relations, 'Gen Z has the lowest financial literacy, study reveals' (19 October 2021), https://mediarelations.gwu.edu/gen-z-has-lowest-financial-literacy-study-reveals, accessed 31 March 2022

Haugen, F, 'Here are 4 key points from the Facebook whistleblower's testimony on Capitol Hill', *NPR* (5 October 2021), www.npr.org/2021/10/05/1043377310/facebook-whistleblower-frances-haugen-congress, accessed 28 March 2022

Heath, D, *Upstream: How to solve problems before they happen* (Bantam Press, 2020)

Holt, J, *How Children Fail*, Revised Edition (Random House, 1982)

Housel, M, *The Psychology of Money: Timeless lessons on wealth, greed and happiness* (Harriman House, 2020)

Jain, N, 'Why you should always bet on dreamers, not experts', *Inc.* (2 September 2014), www.inc.com/naveen-jain/dreamers-vs-the-experts-why-you-should-always-bet-on-dreamers-not-experts.html, accessed 29 March 2022

Jensen, FE with Nutt AE, *The Teenage Brain: A neuroscientist's survival guide to raising adolescents and young adults* (Harper, 2015)

Klapper, L, Lusardi, A and van Oudheusden, P, 'Financial Literacy Around the World', *Standard & Poor's Ratings Services Global Financial Literacy Survey* (2015), https://gflec.org/wp-content/uploads/2015/11/Finlit_paper_16_F2_singles.pdf, accessed 1 April 2022

Lembke, A, *Dopamine Nation: Finding balance in the age of indulgence* (Headline: 2021)

Mann, S, 'Tony Robbins says success is only 20 percent skill – and the rest is all in your head' (28 September 2017), www.inc.com/sonya-mann/tony-robbins-says-entrepreneurship-is-not-for-everyone.html, accessed 1 April 2022

McGrath, M, 'A global financial literacy test finds that just 57% of adults in US are financially literate', *Forbes* (18 November 2015), www.forbes.com/sites/maggiemcgrath/2015/11/18/in-a-global-test-of-financial-literacy-the-u-s, accessed 1 April 2022

National Financial Educators Council, 'Financial illiteracy cost Americans $1,389 in 2021', www.financialeducatorscouncil.org/financial-illiteracy-costs, accessed 28 March 2022

Olen, H, *Pound Foolish: Exposing the dark side of the personal finance industry* (Portfolio, 2012)

Principal Financial Group, 'We make 35,000 decisions per day, but 7 in 10 postpone major financial decisions'

(19 April 2018), www.principal.com/about-us/news -room/news-releases/we-make-35000-decisions-day -7-10-postpone-major-financial-decisions, accessed 30 March 2022

Rock, D, *Your Brain at Work: Strategies for overcoming distraction, regaining focus, and working smarter all day long* (Harper Business, 2009)

Rowe Price, T, *5th Annual Parents, Kids & Money Survey: Detailed results* (March 2013)

Shafir, E and Mullainathan, S, *Scarcity: Why having too little means so much* (Allen Lane, 2013)

Sinek, S, *Start With Why: How great leaders inspire everyone to take action* (Penguin/Portfolio, 2009)

Somanader, T, 'Chart of the week: The persistent gender pay gap', *The White House* (19 September 2014), https://obamawhitehouse.archives.gov/blog/2014/09 /19/chart-week-persistent-gender-pay-gap, accessed 28 March 2022

The Decision Lab, 'Why can we not perceive our own abilities?', https://thedecisionlab.com/biases/dunning -kruger-effect, accessed 29 March 2022

Warren, E and Warren Tyagi, A, *The Two-Income Trap: Why middle-class parents are going broke* (Basic Books, 2004)

Resources

Books

Abeles, V with Rubenstein, G, *Beyond Measure: Rescuing an overscheduled, overtested, underestimated generation* (Simon & Schuster, 2015)

Collins, S, *Neuroscience for Learning and Development: How to apply neuroscience and psychology for improved learning and training* (Kogan Page, 2015)

Cook, J and Priestley, D, *How To Raise Entrepreneurial Kids: Raising confident, resourceful and resilient children who are ready to succeed in life* (Rethink Press, 2020)

Godfrey, J, *Raising Financially Fit Kids* (Ten Speed Press, 2003)

Jay, M, *The Defining Decade: Why your twenties matter and how to make the most of them now* (Twelve, 2012)

Newport, C, *So Good They Can't Ignore You: Why skills trump passion in the quest for work you love* (Business Plus, 2012)

Olen, H and Pollack, H, *The Index Card: Why personal finance doesn't have to be complicated* (Portfolio, 2016)

Robbins, T with Mallouk, P, *Unshakeable: Your financial freedom playbook* (Simon & Schuster, 2017)

Schlesinger, J, *The Dumb Things Smart People Do with Their Money: Thirteen ways to right your financial wrongs* (Ballantine Books, 2019)

The Seven Dollar Millionaire, *Happy Ever After: financial freedom isn't a fairy tale* (Wiley, 2021)

Wagner, T and Dintersmith, T, *Most Likely to Succeed: Preparing our kids for the innovation era* (Scribner, 2016)

Willingham, DT, *Why Don't Students Like School? A cognitive scientist answers questions about how the mind works and what it means for the classroom* (Jossey Bass, 2021)

Zadina, J, *Multiple Pathways to the Student Brain: Energizing and enhancing instruction* (Jossey Bass, 2014)

Articles on financial education programmes

The articles below detail everything parents should look for in a financial education programme and what mistakes they should avoid, and give powerful insights about financial education for teenagers:

Kasman, M, Heuberger, B and Hammond, RA, 'A review of large-scale youth financial literacy education policies and programs'; The Brookings Institution (October 2018), www.brookings.edu/wp-content/uploads/2018/10/ES_20181001_Financial-Literacy-Review.pdf, accessed 1 April 2022

National Scientific Council on the Developing Child, 'Understanding motivation: Building the brain architecture that supports learning, health, and community participation', Harvard University, Working Paper 14 (December 2018), https://developingchild.harvard.edu/resources/understanding-motivation-building-the-brain-architecture-that-supports-learning-health-and-community-participation, accessed 1 April 2022

KFI GLOBAL blogs

Pinto, ML, '3 counterintuitive money mistakes to avoid with your teen' (KFI GLOBAL, 8 February 2021), https://kfi.global/3-counterintuitive-money-mistakes-to-avoid-with-your-teen, accessed 1 April 2022

Pinto, ML, '10 things every parent should know about financial education for teenagers' (KFI GLOBAL, 7 April 2021), https://kfi.global/10-things-every-parent -should-know-about-financial-education-for-teenagers, accessed 1 April 2022

Pinto, ML, 'Teens & money: 7 damaging mistakes parents make' (KFI GLOBAL, 12 April 2021), https:// kfi.global/teens-money-7-damaging-mistakes-parents -make, accessed 1 April 2022

Pinto, ML, '5 attributes of a powerful financial education program for teens' (KFI GLOBAL, 20 April 2021), https://kfi.global/5-attributes-of-a-powerful-financial -education-program-for-teens, accessed 1 April 2022

Pinto, ML, '10 things to look for in a financial education provider' (KFI GLOBAL, 5 May 2021), https://kfi .global/10-things-to-look-for-in-a-financial-education -provider, accessed 1 April 2022

Acknowledgements

I'd like to thank my daughters, Kyra and Lauryn, for keeping me accountable throughout the book-writing process, and my husband Yatin for taking on so much more than was fair, just so I could get on with this.

I am indebted to the rest of my family; their belief in me is what made me step up to this.

I'm grateful to my students, from whom I've learned so much, and it's that learning that's crystallised in this book.

I'd like to especially thank all the parents for trusting me with teaching their kids; their feedback and encouragement meant the world to me.

I'm thankful to the entire KFI team, who's faith in what we do and tenacity in doing it consistently has been the essence of building the methodology described in this book.

A special thanks to my beta readers for their valuable feedback, especially Manisha Daya, Pooja Bhargava, Dana Abusalhieh and Roshni Khanna.

I'd also like to thank my GSD accountability group, Dani Peleva, Vivek Sharma and Matti Hemmi, for their support and encouragement.

The Author

Marilyn Pinto started an education company called KFI GLOBAL five years ago, which specialises in teaching teenagers and young adults how to make smarter money decisions. More than 5,500 students have gone through the KFI financial empowerment programme and are setting themselves up for a financially secure future.

Marilyn works with some of the most respected educational and financial institutions to bring this critical education to more teens across the world. She is on a mission to empower more teenagers with this skill because she believes this will help them step up, stand out and live a life on their own terms.

Marilyn lives in Dubai with her husband and two teenage daughters.

🌐 www.kfi.global

🐦 @kfiglobaltribe

💼 www.linkedin.com/company/kfiglobaltribe

www.ingramcontent.com/pod-product-compliance
Lightning Source LLC
Chambersburg PA
CBHW070541090426
42735CB00013B/3042